44
Questions for
Church Planters

Lyle E. Schaller

Illustrated by **Edward Lee Tucker**

44
Questions for
Church Planters

Abingdon Press
Nashville

To

Bill and Charlotte Maloney

44 QUESTIONS FOR CHURCH PLANTERS

Copyright © 1991 by Abingdon Press

All rights reserved.

This book is printed on acid-free paper.

Library of Congress Cataloging-in-Publication Data

Schaller, Lyle E.
    44 questions for church planters / Lyle E. Schaller ; illustrated by Edward Lee Tucker.
        p.   cm.
    Includes bibliographical references.
    ISBN (invalid) 0-687-13284-2 (alk. paper)
    1. Church development, New.   I. Title. II. Title: Forty four questions for church planters.
BV652.24.S34   1991
254'.1—dc20   90-39764
                                                                                    CIP

MANUFACTURED IN THE UNITED STATES OF AMERICA

Contents

Introduction

It is not an exaggeration to state that it has taken nearly four decades to write this book. The origins go back to the 1951–54 era when this writer was fresh out of the graduate school at the University of Wisconsin and that first permanent job was as a planner in the City Planning Department for the city of Madison, Wisconsin. Among the visitors to that department were pastors and denominational leaders who wanted advice on when and where to start new churches in that rapidly growing metropolitan area.

After a total of seven years in municipal government, graduation from a theological seminary, and a wonderful pastorate with a superb group of parishioners, the next stop was eight and a quarter years as the first director of a cooperative church-planning effort in northeastern Ohio owned by fourteen denominations. This not only provided an exceptional learning experience in polity, politics, and church planning, it also placed a high priority on new church development.

With the assistance of scores of helpful people, most notably the board members of the Regional Church Planning Office plus William and Charlotte Maloney, we were able to study many facets of the Christian churches in urban, suburban, and rural America. Out of those years came a series of forty-seven monographs. The "best seller," co-authored with the Reverend Charles Rawlings, was "Race and Poverty," published in 1964. The fattest was a four-volume census of all of the churches in Summit County, Ohio.

The four monographs that have the greatest relevance to this book were "New Churches in Northeastern Ohio" (1966), "Trends Affecting New Church Development" (1966), "The Coming Crisis in New Church Development" (1967), and "Who Joins a New Mission?" (1968).

That experience was followed by a three-year hitch on the faculty of a theological seminary and two decades on the program staff of a nondenominational retreat center. Every one of the past thirty years has brought new insights through working with leaders responsible for new church development, counseling with new missions, advising denominational committees, research on new congregations and on their constituencies, workshops and seminars with church planters, parish consultations, reading, functioning as an advocate for a greater emphasis on new church development, lectures and interviews with literally thousands of pastors and volunteer leaders in new missions.

A preliminary statement of the reflections and learnings from these experiences was presented eight years ago in a chapter in the book *Growing Plans* (1983).

This book has been written at the urging of Paul Wood and a couple of dozen other church planters and denominational leaders in new church development. Without their insistent harassment plus the encouragement of people like Jack Buteyn, Jeff Spiller, and Mark Platt, this task probably would not have been undertaken. The reader can decide whether they should be thanked or reprimanded for their persistence.

The passage of time often produces hardening of the arteries, hardening of opinions and biases, and a tendency to substitute honesty for tact. The reader will discover this writer has not been immune to the last two of those three tendencies. The only defense that can be offered is the decision not to offer excessive praise in support of (1) the dream of turning the clock back to the era when geographical parishes were considered the norm, (2) telemarketing, (3) that widely shared hope that next year will be 1954, (4) long-term financial subsidies for congregations, or (5) short pastorates.

This book begins with an attempt to respond to that frequently asked question about the need for new churches. The second chapter introduces what this writer believes are the three crucial questions in new church development. Who will be the church planter? What is the vision that drives the effort? Who are the leaders who created that vision? The next two chapters raise three questions that rarely receive the attention they deserve and some will perceive them as diversionary or dull or dumb. Ministers and volunteers who already are engaged in creating a new mission may want to skip these first four chapters and concentrate on some of the more pressing and practical questions that begin with picking a meeting place. That issue is introduced in chapter 5. Overlapping questions on models, target audiences, alternative focal points, and size are raised in chapters 6 and 7.

O GOD, OUR HELP IN AGES PAST, IF ONLY YOU WOULD RETURN US to YESTERYEAR...

Sadly... In church planning there's still a widely shared hope that next year will be 1954!

~ FRIAR TUCK ·

Chapters 8 and 9 reflect a strong bias against the invasion of privacy and contrast telemarketing with direct mail evangelism.

One of the most widely neglected facets of new church development is the value of a distinctive identity for every new mission. Chapter 10 lifts up a dozen questions that will help determine the identity of a new mission.

While neither one receives the deserved attention, two of the early decisions with long-term consequences are (1) the selection of the first volunteer leaders and (2) the place of missions in that new congregation. These are discussed briefly in chapters 11 and 12.

For many people the two central issues in planning new missions are finances and real estate. These are deliberately placed after the discussions of more influential variables such as identity, those initial volunteer leaders, and the place of missions. A half dozen questions on real estate and finances are reviewed in chapter 13.

Sooner or later at least nine out of ten new missions encounter resistance from among some of the pioneers to the goal of continued numerical growth. An extremely biased and one-sided chapter 14 offers a dozen reasons why continued numerical growth is good and should be encouraged.

What proportion of a book on church planting should respond to the concerns of denominational leaders? One answer could be very little since most of the old-line Protestant denominations have sharply reduced their role in new church development. Another response could be a large proportion should be directed to a reversal of that pattern. A third could be very little since the majority of new Protestant churches started in the United States during the 1980s were launched by ministers and lay leaders not related to any denominational agency.

The compromise adopted here has been to allocate approximately 14 percent of the 44 questions and 15 percent of the total pages to a half-dozen issues repeatedly raised by denominational leaders.

A modest, but reasonable goal for every denomination or regional judicatory would be to adopt a "1 percent goal." How many congregations are in your denomination or regional judicatory today? What is 1 percent of that total? That could be your goal. Thus a denomination consisting of 6,000 congregations would seek to start sixty new missions annually. If the goal is substantial growth, that figure should be increased to 2 or 3 percent. In 1970, for example, the Evangelical Free Church included 562 congregations. By 1989 the number of congregations exceeded 1,000. That averaged out to a net increase in the number of congregations of approximately 3.5 percent annually. By exceeding that 1 percent per year pace, the Seventh Day Adventists grew from 3,218 congregations with 420,419 members in 1970 to 4,096 congregations with 675,702 members in 1987. The Wesleyan Church set a goal of slightly over 2 percent annually for the last part of the 1980s. A 2 percent per year pace enabled the Evangelical Lutheran Synod to experience a 40 percent increase in membership between 1970 and 1987. The Wisconsin Evangelical Lutheran Synod averaged a 1.3 percent per year rate in new church development between 1970 and 1987 and thus was able to report a net increase in communicant membership of 17 percent for those seventeen years.

This last chapter has been written for those who are interested in reaching or surpassing that 1 percent goal.

As with earlier volumes in this series the text has been enlivened with a series of cartoons starring Friar Tuck.

CHAPTER ONE

Why Start New Churches?

"This community already is badly overchurched!" declared the pastor of the forty-four-year-old Hillside Church. "I am amazed that you would schedule this meeting to talk about starting one more church out here when most of the existing congregations need more people. We can easily accommodate two hundred people at worship, and we could handle over three hundred by going to two services. Why don't you offer to help us who are out here and struggling to keep our heads above water, rather than spend a lot of money to start another church that isn't needed?"

"That's how I feel," agreed another pastor. "What most of us need is more people, not more competition."

This Tuesday morning meeting had been called by a staff member of a regional judicatory to discuss the plans of that denomination for starting what would be its third church in the east end of that suburban county. First Church had been organized in 1893 and had moved into the present meeting house in 1913 after a fire had completely destroyed its sixteen-year-old white frame building. Shortly after World War II the minister at First Church had taken the initiative in starting what became the Hillside Church and twenty families left First Church to become part of the nucleus for that new mission.

During the past forty years the population in this end of the county had tripled. The Hillside Church reached a peak in size in 1961 with an average attendance of 190, but two successive mismatches in pastors had brought that down sharply. For the past fifteen years the worship attendance at Hillside had averaged between 140 and 160. First Church reached a peak in size in 1956 with an average attendance at worship of slightly over 300, dropped to under 200 in the tumultuous sixties, but was now back up to nearly 300 in church on Sunday morning.

HM-M-M... THERE ARE ALWAYS BIGGER CROWDS OUTSIDE THAN WITHIN!

'Everywhere...more folks are unchurched than there are churches to fill their needs!

— FRIAR TUCK

The missions committee for that regional judicatory had concluded the time had come to start another new church in this area and had asked this staff person to meet with these two pastors plus any other ministers from other churches who might be interested in discussing this subject.

"I came here in 1982," explained Pastor Paul Schultz, "and at least a dozen new congregations have been organized since then. One of them went bankrupt about a year after the members moved into their new building and they had to sell their property to another church that bought it as part of their plan to become a multi-site congregation. Unless you have enough money to subsidize a new mission for at least six or eight years, I would suggest you not try it. All the good church sites have been developed, so now you have a choice between either poor locations or exorbitant prices for land that already has buildings on it."

"I wish you would tell us why your committee chose this area for a new mission," persisted the pastor from the Hillside Church. "What were they thinking? Why pick an area that already is over-churched?"

Before suggesting an answer to what appears to be a rational, logical, and relevant question, it may be useful to look briefly at three slices of American church history.

That First Big Era

Back in 1793 President Ezra Stiles of Yale University predicted that a century later the population of this new nation would be divided equally among the Congregationalists, Presbyterians, and Anglicans.

Less than thirty years later, in 1820, the Methodists and the Baptists each reported approximately 2,700 congregations in the United States. The Presbyterians were in third place with 1,700 congregations followed by the Congregationalists with 1,100 and the Lutherans with 800. The Episcopalians were sixth with 600 parishes, and a half-dozen other denominations reported a combined total of slightly over 1,300 churches for a grand total of nearly 11,000 congregations.[1] This averaged out to one religious congregation for every 875 of the 9.6 million residents of this new nation.

THE HILLS ARE ALIVE WITH THE SOULS OF MILLIONS!

NEW CHURCHES FOR A NEW NATION

In the beginning, there was no reluctance over starting new churches!

—FRIAR TUCK.

Forty years later, in 1860, the number of churches had increased fivefold to approximately 54,000 while the population had more than tripled to 31.5 million.[2] This produced a ratio of one congregation for every 600 residents, about the same ratio that has persisted for most of the next thirteen decades. It should be noted that religious congregations were even more fragile in the nineteenth century than they are today. Many were born every day, but a substantial proportion did not survive for as long as a decade, and the life expectancy of scores of new congregations was counted in weeks or months, not years. The appearance of a magnetic preacher often gave birth to a new church, but some faded away shortly after that itinerant minister disappeared from the scene. At least one-third, and probably closer to one-half or more of those 54,000 churches in existence in 1860 were not around to be counted in the census of religious bodies taken in 1906.

Another way of stating that is in the two-hundred forty years following the landing of the Pilgrims at Plymouth Rock, a total of 54,000 congregations were established that were still in existence in 1860. During the next thirty years the number of religious congregations tripled from 54,000 in 1860 to 165,151 in 1890.

By 1906 the number of Methodist churches (64,701) and the number of Baptist congregations (54,880) each exceeded the total number of churches back in 1860.

Of the 212,230 religious bodies counted in 1906, at least one-half were less than thirty years old. Even in such a long-established denomination as the Congregational Church, one-half of the 5,713 churches in existence in 1906 had been founded during the previous thirty years. As might be expected, one-half of all Lutheran parishes in 1906 had yet to celebrate their twenty-third birthday. Even the Protestant Episcopal Church, which was not known for its aggressiveness in launching new missions, reported in 1906 that nearly one-half of its parishes had been in existence for fewer than thirty years. Nearly three out of five Presbyterian congregations were under forty years of age in 1906.*

Between 1860 and 1906 the population of the United States increased from 31.5 million to 85.4 million, and the number of churches nearly quadrupled from 54,000 to over 212,000. That represented one additional congregation for every increase of 350 in the population. Approximately 85 percent of that net increase in the number of churches was accounted for by eight denominational families. The fifteen Methodist denominations reported a combined net increase of approximately 45,000 congregations, the sixteen Baptist groups more than quadrupled with a net increase of 42,700 churches, the Lutherans added 10,500 parishes, the Roman Catholics reported a net increase of slightly over 10,000 parishes, the twelve Presbyterian bodies reported a combined net gain of nearly 9,000 congregations, the Disciples of Christ quadrupled with a net gain of 6,200 churches, and the Protestant Episcopal Church experienced a net gain of 4,700 parishes while the Congregationalists reported a net increase of nearly 3,500 churches.

Between 1899 and 1906 the population increased by nine million, and at least 32,000 new churches were organized—an average of one new congregation for every increase of 280 in the population.[3]

---

*When the new Evangelical Lutheran Church in America came into existence in 1988, approximately one-half of all participating parishes had been in existence for at least seven decades. Of the 37,500 congregations in The United Methodist Church in 1990, at least 30,000 were founded before 1940.

By contrast, during the 1980s the population of the United States increased by 24 million, and the number of churches increased by an estimated 35,000 or one additional religious body for every 685 net increase in the population. A more conservative estimate is a *net* increase of only 25,000 churches during the 1980s, since an estimated 30,000 congregations ceased to exist sometime during the 1980s. That would be the equivalent of one *new* congregation for every *net* increase of 435 in the nation's population and one *additional* religious body for

WOW!... FOLKS ARE FILL-IN 'EM AS FAST AS WE CAN BUILD 'EM!

History shows: church growth was matched by church building!
—FRIAR TUCK

every increase of 960 people in the total population.

For Lutheran readers it may be interesting to note that during the 1890s, when the population of the United States increased by 13 million, the two dozen Lutheran denominations organized at least 2,626 new parishes, an average of one new mission for every increase of 5,000 in the nation's population. During the 1980s the population of the United States increased by 24 million and the twenty Lutheran bodies organized a combined total of approximately 1,600 new missions or one for every increase of 15,000 in the population.

The predecessor denominations of today's Presbyterian Church (U.S.A.) organized well over 2,000 new congregations during the 1890s, 200 of which were African-American churches. During the ten years of 1979–1988 the Presbyterian Church in the United States and the United Presbyterian Church in the United States of America together organized a combined total of 571 new missions. The Protestant Episcopal Church organized 1,111 new missions during the 1890s that were still in existence in 1906.

The six predecessor denominations of today's United Methodist Church organized a combined total of 6,946 new congregations during the 1890s, down from the 7,395 during the 1880s.

The Northern Methodists led this effort, organizing more than one-half of their 29,943 congregations of 1906 during the 1870–1906 period including 3,750 African-American churches with a combined membership of nearly one-third of a million. During the 1980s The United Methodist Church organized fewer than 700 new churches.

Black Methodists were nearly as busy as the whites in organizing new congregations in the post-Civil War era. The African Methodist Church reported that an average of more than two new churches were organized every week during the 1870–1906 period with 1,091 started in the seven years of 1900–1906 inclusive. The AME Zion Church reported that over one-half of their 2,204 congregations were organized from 1880 through 1906 as were one-half of the 2,381 congregations affiliated with the Colored Methodist Episcopal Church.

For another perspective one can point out that between 1820 and 1860 the number of congregations affiliated with one of the various Methodist denominations increased by 17,000. In the forty years following the end of the Civil War, the net increase in Methodist congregations of all branches of that Wesleyan tradition grew by 47,000, nearly triple the 1820–40 pace.

During the first fifty years of its existence (1852–1903), the Congregational Church Building Society offered financial assistance to 3,491 new congregations. The American Missionary Association organized more than 150 new Negro congregations after the Civil War, many of which were organized around a Christian day school.

The Congregationalists organized 1,074 new congregations during the 1890s while the two predecessors of the Evangelical and Reformed Church launched a combined total of 396 (down from 419 during the 1880s). The Disciples of Christ organized 1,953 new churches during the 1880s, but still slower than their subsequent pace when they started 2,122 new churches during the seven years of 1900 through 1906.

The 1890s turned out to be the peak decade for new church development for the Northern Baptists as they organized 1,255 new congregations, up by seven over the 1880s. The Southern Baptist Convention was gearing up for a faster pace as they recorded 3,316 new churches during the 1880s, 3,576 during the

1890s, and 3,893 in the seven-year period of 1900 through 1906.

Two-thirds of the 18,543 churches affiliated with the National Baptist Convention in 1906 were started during the 1870–1899 period with 4,163 reporting their organizational date as being in the 1890s.

Between 1820 and 1860 the number of Baptist churches in America increased by nearly 10,000 to 12,150. During the next forty-six years that grand total quadrupled to 54,880 in 1906—one-half of which were organized in the twenty-seven years from 1880 through 1906.

GRACIOUS, THEY'RE BUILDING A NEW CHURCH WHILE THEY CAN STILL SEE *the* STEEPLE *of* THE LAST ONE!

From 1860 to 1900, while the land's population doubled, new churches grew four-fold!
— FRIAR TUCK.

During those twenty-seven years the population of the United States increased from 50.3 million to 85.4 million. The number of Baptist churches doubled while the nation's population grew by 70 percent.

The big increase in the wave of independent or "nondenom-inational" churches that have become such a highly visible feature of the contemporary ecclesiastical landscape can be traced back to the turn of the century. Four out of five of the 1,079 independent congregations counted in that religious census of 1906 came into existence after 1880, and 734 were organized in the 1890–1906 era.

For most of what are sometimes called the "old-line" Protestant denominations, the half century between the end of the Civil War and the beginning of World War I represented their peak efforts in organizing new churches. It also should be noted here that the figures used to report the number of new churches organized during this era understate reality since (a) 15 percent of all congregations did not report their date of organization in that 1906 census of religious bodies and (b) some congregations organized in the 1870s, 1880s, and 1890s obviously were no longer in existence when the census of 1906 was taken.

A Threefold Strategy

A few readers may find this brief, historical detour to be interesting while others may wonder about its relevance. This statistical review is offered to document two-thirds of the threefold strategy traditionally used by the old-line Protestant denominations to reach new generations of Americans. One component of that strategy reached a peak during the five decades between the end of the Civil War and the beginning of World War I. That was to reach more people by organizing hundreds of thousands of new churches. It continues to be the most useful and productive component of any denominational church growth strategy.

A second, and overlapping part of that strategy, was to increase the number of churches per 10,000 population. In 1860, the United States reported one Protestant church for every 610 residents, compared to one church for every 875 residents in 1820. Between 1860 and 1906 the Roman Catholic population of the United States quadrupled to 14 million, but the ratio of Protestant churches to the total population increased to one for every 430 total population.

The third component of what may have been an informal or unofficial strategy blossomed during the first six or seven decades of the twentieth century. This was to increase the size of the average congregation. Between 1906 and 1970 the average (mean) size of the congregations in several denominations doubled or tripled. This growth in the average size of congregations coincided with (a) the continued numerical growth in several denominations and (b) the gradual reduction in the number of new congregations organized each year. While it is impossible to prove a cause-and-effect relationship, the evidence suggests (a) that rapid increase in the number of new congregations was the most influential single factor in the numerical growth of scores of denominations and (b) that subsequent increase in the average size of congregations at least partially offset that drop in the numbers of new missions launched each year since World War II.

Table I

CHURCH-MEMBERSHIP RATIOS

Average (mean) number of members per congregation

Denomination	1906	1970	1988
American Baptist Churches	128	242	269
Chr. Ch. (Disciples of Christ)	120	178	169
Christian Reformed Church	132	234	212
Episcopal Church	132	312	235
Ev. Lutheran Ch. in America*	167	365	350
L.D.S. (Mormons)	197	351	378
Lutheran Church-Mo. Synod	161	350	332
Presbyterian Church (U.S.A.)*	132	319	252
Reformed Church in America	197	243	220
Roman Catholic Church	975	2035	2275
Seventh Day Adventist	33	131	165
Southern Baptist Convention	95	339	395
United Church of Christ*	149	291	258
United Methodist Church*	93	262	236

*Combined for predecessor denominations

Our first strategy was to meet new people with new churches!

— FRIAR TUCK

Our second strategy: Build new churches faster than the population's growth!

— FRIAR TUCK

Smaller and Fewer

The third slice of American church history that is a part of the context for responding to questions about the rationale for organizing new churches includes two facets. Both should be examined in the light of two generalizations. The first is the second law of thermodynamics which, when translated into institutional terms, states that sooner or later everything runs down.[4] Thus the normal and predictable pattern is for congregations gradually to shrink in size. This principle also has been used by historians and political scientists to explain the rise and fall of nations. While it always is dangerous to rely on any single factor of analysis for an explanation of a complex pattern, entropy does help explain some recent trends.[5]

Another useful generalization is that new churches are more likely to reach more people and to grow in size than are long-established parishes.[6] Perhaps the simplest explanation of this pattern is that new congregations are organized around evangelism and reaching people not actively involved in the life of any worshiping community. By contrast, powerful internal institutional pressures tend to encourage long-established churches to allocate most of their resources to the care of members. One result is that the vast majority of new congregations in the United States reach their peak in size during the first two or three decades of their existence and then remain on a plateau in size or begin to shrink in numbers.

TO KEEP FROM FAILING WE LEARNED TO BUILD-UP OUR RESERVES!

Our third strategy: Increase the size of our congregations!

—FRIAR TUCK

These two generalizations shed some light on the statistics in Table I. For several denominations that rapid increase in the average size of congregations reached a peak in the 1960s or early 1970s before it began to reverse itself. This is more obvious in the figures for long-established denominations such as the Presbyterian Church (U.S.A.), the United Church of Christ, The United Methodist Church, and the Episcopal Church. That pattern is not represented in the figures for several newer and more evangelistic religious bodies such as the Southern Baptist Convention, the Seventh Day Adventists, and the Latter Day Saints (Mormons).

The second trend is reported in Table II. This reports the decline in both the number of congregations and in the number of members of several of the old-line Protestant denominations. While no one can prove the cause-and-effect relationships, it appears that a decrease in congregations and in membership naturally go together unless that denomination also experiences a sharp increase in the size of the average congregation.

Taken together these two tables suggest that the decrease in the number of congregations for several denominations during the first six or seven decades of the twentieth century was partly a result of entropy and partly a predictable product of that cutting back in the efforts to organize new congregations. (The extent of

Table II

NUMBER OF CONGREGATIONS AND MEMBERS

Denomination	1906		1970		1987	
	Congregations	Members	Congregations	Members	Congregations	Members
American Baptist Churches	8,272	1,052,105	6,090	1,472,478	5,864	1,576,483
Christian Church (Disciples)	8,293	982,701	5,114	911,964	4,195	718,552
Christian Reformed	174	26,669	660	154,276	682	225,951
Ev. Lutheran Church in America	N.A.	N.A.	10,900	4,100,000	11,113	3,952,663
Episcopal Church	6,845	886,942	7,069	2,208,773	7,387	1,741,036
LDS (Mormons)	501	40,851	4,828	1,695,793	8,682	3,280,000
Lutheran Church-Missouri Synod	3,301	648,529	5,690	1,922,569	5,912	1,973,347
Presbyterian Church (U.S.A.)	12,150	1,600,000	12,673	4,045,408	11,513	2,967,781
Reformed Church in America	659	124,938	923	224,170	925	203,581
Roman Catholic Church	12,482	12,079,142	23,708	48,214,729	23,552	53,496,862
Seventh Day Adventists	1,889	62,211	3,218	420,419	4,096	675,702
Southern Baptist Conv.	21,104	2,009,471	34,340	11,628,032	37,238	14,722,617
United Church of Christ	8,654	1,296,271	6,727	1,960,608	6,395	1,662,568
United Methodist Church	57,087	5,252,607	40,654	10,671,774	37,773	9,055,000

Note: In order to secure a reasonable degree of comparability this table is limited to those religious bodies identified as separate denominations in the *Census of Religious Bodies: 1906.* Current denominational names are used. For earlier years the statistics for the predecessor denominations are combined. The sharp decline in the numbers for the Christian Church (Disciples of Christ) is in part a result of the changed definition of member congregations. The 1970 statistics for the Evangelical Lutheran Church in America include an estimate for the Association of Evangelical Lutheran Churches. The methodology used in reporting statistics in the Roman Catholic Church means these figures are not directly comparable to Protestant statistics. The statistics for both the American Baptist Churches and the Southern Baptist Convention include congregations with a dual affiliation with another Baptist denomination. The membership figures reported in the *Census of Religious Bodies: 1906* do not include every one of the congregations of that denomination, but that is a minor factor. The 1906 statistics for the United Church of Christ represent the combined total for the Congregationalists, the Reformed Church in the United States, and the German Evangelical Synod of North America.

this cut-back can be illustrated by four examples. In the three-year period of 1959–61 the United Church of Christ started an average of 44 new churches annually. In the 1969–71 period that average had dropped to three new churches a year. The American Lutheran Church organized 315 new parishes in the 1960–64 era and 115 in the 1975–79 period. The Methodist Church organized 176 new churches in 1961, while The United Methodist Church started 16 new missions in 1971. The predecessors of The Presbyterian Church (U.S.A.) launched 116 new congregations in 1960 compared to 25 in 1972, 34 in 1973, and 27 in 1974.)

Those two factors were more than offset, however, by that sharp increase in the average size of congregations. During the past two decades the sharper cutbacks in planting new churches and the decrease in the average size of long-established congregations meant that a numerical decline in membership was inevitable in several denominations.

To state it even more simply, every denomination is limited to a pair of alternatives when the goal is to increase membership. One is to increase the size of existing congregations—and that runs against the normal, predictable, and powerful forces of institutional behavior. Fewer than 1 percent of the 350,000 to 400,000 Protestant churches in the United States average a thousand or more at Sunday morning worship. That is at least four times the total in 1950. If those figures can be used to predict the future, they suggest the odds are only one in a hundred that a given congregation will reach that size. For several of the old-line Protestant denominations that ratio is closer to one in five hundred churches that average a thousand or more at worship. This is especially significant for those denominations that seek to reach the generations of people born after 1955 since they can be found in disproportionately large numbers in (a) new congregations and (b) very large churches.

If the goal is to reach more people, the only alternative to larger congregations is to increase the number of churches. Six of the denominations listed in Table II have experienced a decrease in the number of congregations, and four of the six also report a decrease in the average size of their congregations.

When faced with these two choices, most denominational

IT TAKES ENORMOUS EFFORT *for* AN ESTABLISHED CHURCH *to* GROW *from* WITHIN*!*

GRUNT!
SIGH!

Churches which start small have little desire to grow!
— *FRIAR TUCK*

officials will admit there is little they can do to increase the size of their long-established congregations.* That leaves the alternative of increasing the number of churches affiliated with that denomination. That goal can be accomplished by (a) annexing independent churches that seek a denominational affiliation and/or (b) facilitating the division of existing congregations so one becomes two and/or (c) planting new missions.

That is what this book is about, and these introductory pages are designed to provide part of the context for the first of these 44 questions.

Why Plant More Churches?

Most parents have learned the hard way that a simple and single-faceted answer rarely is acceptable to everyone when a complex and awesome question is raised that begins with the three-letter word, "Why?" That also is true for this discussion. Why start more churches? At least a dozen responses can be offered to that crucial question. It is reasonable to assume that no one answer will be a satisfactory explanation for everyone. It also is safe to assume that some opponents of church planting will not be persuaded by this combination of a dozen different reasons.

---

*The only religious bodies that have substantial control over whether existing congregations will grow substantially in size are those in which a denominational executive can control ministerial placement. The prime Protestant example of this policy is The United Methodist Church. That denomination illustrates that (a) episcopal control over ministerial placement does not guarantee an increase in the size of long-established congregations (see Table I) and (b) the needs of the clergy may take precedence over numerical growth.

For many Christians the central argument in support of planting new churches is to be found in the Great Commission (Matt. 28:18-20). Through the centuries the response to the Great Commission has included (a) the ministry of itinerant evangelists, (b) the creation of a huge variety of movements, organizations, and orders that can be grouped under the term "parachurch movements," (c) the organization of Christian institutions such as congregations, missionary sending agencies, denominations, elementary schools, high schools, social service agencies, youth minis-

GULP! SHE WANTS OUT!

Established churches have a tough time attracting young people!
—FRIAR TUCK

tries, retreat centers, camps, orphanages, colleges, universities, theological seminaries, and hospitals, (d) the recruitment, training, and sending of missionaries to other parts of this planet, (e) the translation and worldwide distribution of the Holy Scriptures, (f) the gathering together of small groups of people completely unrelated to any institutional expression of the Christian church, and (g) the founding of intentional communities of Christians committed to living out their faith together. But number one on this list of responses to the Great Commission has always been the creation of new worshiping communities called congregations or parishes or missions or churches. Throughout the centuries this has been the most common attempt to obey that directive of Jesus to make disciples from among those who have been living outside the faith. For some that is the only legitimate and the only necessary answer to that question of Why?

The more pragmatic may turn to the historical record summarized earlier in this chapter and explain, "Planting new churches is the closest we have to a guaranteed means of reaching more people with the Good News that Jesus Christ is Lord and

ALAS, IT WILL BE EASIER FOR OUR PASTOR TO BUY A NEW CAR THAN FOR OUR CHURCH to ATTRACT NEW MEMBERS!

PASTOR'S RESIDENCE

Often, the needs of the pastor take precedence over those of the church!
—FRIAR TUCK

Savior." The historical record is clear that we cannot rely on long-established congregations to reach all the new generations of people.

A third, and perhaps overlapping reason, is that historically new congregations have turned out to be the most effective approach to reaching new generations of people. This is an operational expression of the old cliche, "Create new groups for new people." To state it in personal terms, parents born before 1945 should support planting new churches as part of a larger strategy to retain the adult children of those parents in that denominational family.

A fourth, and far more subtle explanation, centers on the word "different." A different order of worship, a different approach to proclaiming the faith, and a different style of ministry can be more effective in reaching people outside the church than that used to service the already committed Christians. Scores of new missions have declared the secret of their success in reaching the unchurched is a result of a different approach to ministry. They contend that a worship service designed for already committed believers seldom will be meaningful to those with no background in the Christian faith. This generalization applies to the design of that worship experience, the choice of hymns, the content of the sermon, the place of instrumental music, the reading of Scripture, the announcements, the proclamation of the faith, the prayers, and the benediction. Dozens even go so far as to offer every week one worship experience for the unchurched and new believers and another and a substantially different worship service designed for believers. This approach to ministry contrasts sharply with at least a few long-established churches that assume one worship service on Sunday morning can be a meaningful experience for both the believers, regardless of the stage of their religious pilgrimage, and for the curious non-believers.

OH! OH! IT'S THE EVER-FORWARD FLICK OF THE FAITH!

The great Commission is still the basis for building churches and adding members!

—FRIAR TUCK

While some readers may rank it lower in their value system, a fifth reason for planting new missions is to reach those venturesome personalities who enjoy helping pioneer the new. Often these people, many of whom are church shoppers, feel rejected or unwanted or bored or superfluous when they go to the long-established congregation that places a premium on tradition, tenure, routine, kinship ties, experience, legalisms, and the past and disdains creativity, innovation, risk, and a strong future-orientation. This also can be a powerful attraction to some self-identified Christians who "dropped out" of church years earlier and thus often are classified as "unchurched."

Overlapping this is a sixth factor that often is articulated by newer members of a new mission. They perceive the new church they recently joined as focused largely on two words: "evangelism" and "mission." They support that emphasis. They are convinced both are central to a biblical definition of a worshiping community. By contrast, they often point to long-established congregations as being excessively self-centered and overly concerned with institutional survival goals and/or functioning as adult employment centers for people in need of a job.

A seventh reason has been documented repeatedly and several denominations have made it a major consideration in their strategy for new church development. Contrary to conventional wisdom, congregations usually benefit from intradenominational competition. While it is impossible to isolate one factor as being decisive, the presence of two or more congregations with the same denomina-

SOMETHING DIFFERENT
IS OFTEN NEEDED
TO ATTRACT MORE
THAN THE
SAME OLD CROWD!

New ventures bring-out
the venturesome!

— FRIAR TUCK.

tional affiliation usually results in a higher level of congregational health and vitality than if one congregation has a denominational monopoly in that community. One obvious advantage of that system of intentional redundancy is that discontented members of one congregation can seek a new church home without leaving that denomination. This also is one of several arguments used in opposition to intradenominational congregational mergers as well as in support of planting new missions.

An eighth argument is based on the simple assumption that no one congregation possesses the skills and can muster the resources necessary to reach, attract, serve, and be responsive to the needs of every resident. The simplest expression of this argument goes something like this: "We already have two congregations in that community. One is well to the left of the center of the theological spectrum and the other is right in the middle. Let's find an evangelical pastor who will organize a new congregation to reach that theologically more conservative segment of the population."

Another expression of the same argument is to plan for one congregation that will be able to welcome those young religious pilgrims who were reared in the Roman Catholic Church, a second that can serve mature adults, a third that will be designed around a variety of ministries with parents of young children, and a fourth that will focus on social justice.

This argument is repugnant to those who believe that every congregation can and should live out Paul's admonition to be all things to all people (I Cor. 9:19-23). That goal often is beyond the resources or the preferences of most congregations.

While this is opposed by those who strongly believe that new immigrants should be assimilated into existing institutions as quickly as possible, a strong argument in the 1890s and the 1990s for planting new churches was and is to reach the new immigrants to this nation. This argument appears to have wider support in Canada than in the United States today. Clearly it had stronger support in the 1880s than in the closing decades of the twentieth century. That difference can be documented by contrasting the number of new foreign language missions started by Lutherans, Presbyterians, Methodists, and the Reformed denominations a century ago with parallel efforts today.

I JUST KNOW THIS WILL HELP MY CIRCULATION AND PERIPHERAL VISION!

Intradenominational competition creates better congregational health and vitality!
— FRIAR TUCK

Today the Southern Baptist Convention stands out as the number one example of a denominational commitment to plant new missions to reach new immigrants. The Conservative Baptist Association, the Salvation Army, and the new Evangelical Lutheran Church in America are other examples of that policy.

A tenth argument occasionally offered for starting new churches is to "reach our people who have moved out there." This was one of the two or three most common explanations behind that wave of new church development in the 1946–65 era, but is heard far less frequently today as fewer people select a church on the basis of geographical convenience. Today this explanation is most often used as Southern Baptists organize new congregations in the Midwest and in New England, as the United Church of Christ and the Reformed Church in America launch new missions in the Sunbelt, and as the Roman Catholic Church starts new missions in what once was the Bible Belt and in the northern suburbs.

One of the most powerful arguments for planting new churches is seldom articulated and has three facets to it. The

O GOD, FOR THOSE WHO HAVEN'T FOUND A PLACE IN THIS PLACE, WE ASK THAT YOU PLACE THEM IN A PLACE OF YOUR OWN CHOOSING...

There is a need for different churches for differing people!

— FRIAR TUCK

central argument is that starting new churches can be an effective means of changing the denominational mix.

Five outstanding examples of that argument are the Southern Baptist Convention, the Seventh Day Adventists, the Roman Catholic Church, the Lutheran Church-Missouri Synod, and the Jehovah's Witnesses. Each of what once was an all-Anglo denomination has used new church development as a means of becoming a more inclusive religious body. Parallel efforts are currently underway in the Assemblies of God, the Evangelical Lutheran Church in America, the American Baptist Churches in the U.S.A., the Reformed Church in America, The United Methodist Church, and the United Church of Christ.

(This may be the place to note that most efforts by predominantly Anglo denominations to organize new missions in what are largely African-American neighborhoods in the central city and older suburbs usually produce one of eight results: [1] a numerically growing congregation in which the common denominator is the strong upward mobility desire of parents for their children, [2] a growing congregation that reflects the African-American religious subculture more than the culture and traditions of that predominantly Anglo denomination, [3] a highly liturgical worship experience that usually is accompanied by moderate growth, [4] a heavily subsidized ministry that does not achieve either the financial or the numerical goals that were articulated when the new ministry was launched, [5] a heavily subsidized ministry organized largely around social welfare programs, advocacy, and a "Christian presence," with only a modest emphasis on building a worshiping community, [6] a growing congregation drawn largely from lower income residents that is effectively organized around the capability of the preacher to communicate the transformational power of the gospel [Matt. 11:4-5] *and the lives of the people are transformed,* [7] a numerically growing congregation organized around the combination of worship, music, a Christian day school, and the personality of the pastor, or [8] the combination of a predominantly female worshiping community and a social welfare program designed to serve residents of public housing. It also should be noted that some of these efforts by predominantly Anglo denominations to organize new congregations in African-American neighborhoods may be perceived by African-American pastors as colonial ventures by well-financed outsiders designed to "cream off" the best male leaders, the most generous contributors, and the active upwardly mobile members from the existing African-American churches as part of a larger effort to alleviate white guilt.)

The second facet of changing the denominational mix is illustrated by those with an aging membership such as the Presbyterian Church (U.S.A.), The United Methodist Church, and the Christian Church (Disciples of Christ). Each could use an extensive church planting program as a means of reaching younger generations of people and thus lower that rising median age of the membership. That argument for organizing more new churches does not win easy and widespread support! Many of the aging congregations oppose such efforts on the grounds that all available resources should be utilized to channel new generations of younger potential members to existing churches, not into new missions.

Since the vast majority of the large and rapidly growing new Protestant churches in North America tend to be located on the conservative half of that theological spectrum, a third facet of this argument would be for the liberal Protestant denominations to sharply increase the number of new missions organized by a theologically conservative pastor.

Occasionally a regional judicatory will use a new congregation as a laboratory or experimental venture to try out other new ideas that could change the denominational mix. In several cases this has been to test the values of visual communication in worship.

During the 1960s and 1970s new church development was one method of testing the concept of interdenominational or

HI... WELCOME TO AMERICA!
WE'RE STARTING A NEW
CHURCH AND...

Today's approach
to new church growth
duplicates successful past
efforts with immigrants!

—FRIAR TUCK·)

interracial or intercultural congregations or "house churches"[7] or shopping mall churches. The net results of these experiments demonstrated (a) few Roman Catholics are interested in being part of an "ecumenical church" (the big exception being charismatic fellowships), (b) a shopping mall can be a high cost means of creating a small congregation, (c) house churches and numerical growth usually are incompatible, (d) if the goal is to reach large numbers of people, carry either one denominational affiliation or none, not two (the big exceptions are dual affiliation African-American congregations or churches affiliated with different denominations on different continents), (e) the fuzzier the identity, the smaller the number of people who seek out that church will be, and (f) sooner or later nearly every congregation wants and needs its own permanent meeting place.

This concept of designing new missions to test new concepts of missions can be a third way to change the mixture of people, ideas, approaches to ministry, models of congregational life, and style of corporate worship within one denomination. It is easier to experiment with new ideas in a new setting than in a long-established organization where tradition, culture, past experiences, and customs make it difficult for innovation to get a fair test.

Finally, for those who can endorse denominations as legitimate orders of God's creation, who are open to simple pragmatic pleas, and who also have a sense of history, a twelfth argument can be offered, "If we don't, someone else will."

To state it even more simply, in any community in which (a) a substantial proportion of the residents do not go to any church and/or (b) there is a significant turnover in the population year after year and/or (c) the number of residents is increasing, new churches will be organized. This is one of the lessons of American church history documented earlier. The number of congregations will rise as the population grows. Newcomers will provide an attractive justification for someone to plant a new church. The existence of those residents who do not go to any church will challenge some church planters.

Back in the 1950s and 1960s many of the denominational leaders of that era subscribed to a concept called comity.[8] Comity turned out to be a means of (a) minimizing the number of congregations organized by the participating denominations, (b) perpetuating the obsolete dream that people choose a church on the basis of its geographical proximity to their place of residence, (c) undercutting the attraction of denominational affiliation, (d) reinforcing the ancient notion that every congregation should have its meeting place located at the center of what would be a geographical parish, rather than in a highly visible and easily accessible location, (e) forcing the more ambitious but loyal participants to choose second-rate locations, and (f) leaving open to non-partici-

WE WE'RE NEVER THIS OPEN UNTIL SEVERAL NEW CHURCHES THREATENED TO CLOSE US!

New churches make many denominations more inclusive!

— FRIAR TUCK

New ideas work better in newer settings!

— FRIAR TUCK

35

FEWER CHURCHES CAN ONLY MAKE US MORE EASILY IGNORED!

To limit the number of new churches could prove to be counter-productive!

—FRIAR TUCK

IF WE DON'T DO IT, SOMEONE ELSE WILL!

Newcomers . . . are often reason enough for starting a new church!

—FRIAR TUCK

pating churches many of the most attractive sites for new missions. In other words, efforts to freeze the number of congregations in a community or to limit the number of new congregations in a community or to limit the number of new churches have been ineffective. In recent years several municipalities have used their land-use controls to limit the expansion of existing churches and to bar the creation of new congregations, but these restrictions are under legal attack as violations of the First and Fifth Amendments to the Constitution of the United States of America.[9] For long-established congregations to support these municipal restrictions as part of a larger strategy to freeze the number of churches, reduce intercongregational competition, and preserve the status quo, could, in the long run, turn out to be counterproductive behavior.

While they will not persuade everyone, those are some of the reasons why a central component of any evangelistic strategy should be to plant new churches. Those who are categorically opposed to that strategy may want to look at adoptions and divisions as an alternative, but that raises two questions that deserve a new chapter.

CHAPTER TWO

Three Crucial Variables

Some new congregations begin with a large crowd of enthusiastic people and continue to grow year after year and decade after decade. Many more soon reach a plateau in size and level off with an average Sunday morning worship attendance of one hundred forty or less. Others expand their numbers rapidly for a few years, reach a peak in size, and then experience a decade or two of gradual numerical decline.

What is the difference? Why does one new congregation continue to win many new members while another, that meets in a building only a few miles away, plateaus in size prematurely? Is there a magic formula for guaranteeing success in new church development?

One response to that question has been to concentrate on a carefully designed survey of the residents of that community to enable those responsible for planting that new church to design it to match the needs of those residents. Another has been to send in a team of three to five full-time people to plant that new church. A third has been to purchase the ideal parcel of land at the perfect location, regardless of the cost, as part of a larger design in new church development. A fourth has been to guarantee the new mission financial subsidies for the first five to ten years. A fifth has been to enlist individual congregations to serve as sponsoring churches and to "mother" or nurture new missions. A sixth has been to prepare a comprehensive manual for church planters on what to do and how to do it and require all prospective mission-developer pastors to complete a two- or three-week training program using that manual as the textbook. A seventh has been to build a staff of denominational specialists with a high level of competence in overseeing new church development. An eighth has been to recruit and train a cadre of church planters who accept this specialized role and become

OOPS! THERE GOES THE NEIGHBORHOOD!

THIS IS THE SITE of A NEW CHURCH!

New churches tend to grow faster than established churches!

— FRIAR TUCK

itinerant developers of new missions. Typically, they come in and organize a new congregation. Two to five years later they depart to plant a new church in some other promising place.

What Works Best?

While each of those eight alternative approaches to planting a new mission has merit, they are not offered here as a comprehensive or exhaustive list of possibilities. Far more important, none of the eight stands out as the best approach.

Experience suggests the best way to start a new church that will attract a large cadre of enthusiastic charter members and continue to grow in numbers year after year is to identify the right person to be the mission-developer pastor and for that minister to continue as the pastor for a minimum of twenty-five years. Choosing and retaining the right pastor clearly is the key variable in planting a new mission that will continue decade after decade to challenge an ever-growing number of people with the Good News that Jesus Christ is Lord and Savior. Ideally the criteria used in making that selection of a church planter will be consistent with the vision (see next section of this chapter) that is the motivating force behind the decision to launch this new mission.

It is difficult to believe that anyone who has studied the past fifty years of new church development on the North American continent would challenge that assertion. If the selection and retention of the pastor is the key variable, why has so much effort been expended on other factors such as the use of telemarketing, surveying the nearby residents to discover their wants, preparing exhaustive manuals on techniques for planting new churches, raising large sums of money to subsidize new missions, designing workshops for church planters, and encouraging churches to sponsor new missions?

Five Reasons

One reason for overlooking or down-playing the crucial importance of that mission developer's role is a natural reluctance to support what often is described by its critics as the "cult of the personality." Many prefer to believe that the clergy should be seen as a batch of interchangeable parts. This ideological position is based on the assumption that no pastor is indispensable. One pastor should be able to succeed another without any significant disruption in the ongoing life of that worshiping community. This functional view of the parish ministry tends to minimize the importance of relationships. Some people join a particular congregation because they like the pastor. Others do not return after their first visit because they were unfavorably impressed with that same pastor.

The dream that any fully credentialed minister can effectively serve any congregation has practically no overlap with contemporary reality. The fear of the consequences of building a new congregation around the gifts, personality, skills, priorities, and approach to ministry of one long-tenured pastor is a concern that perhaps can best be discussed in terms of tradeoffs. Which do you prefer? Creating what will become a large and vital congregation able to offer a vast range of ministries and specialized programs in response to the varying needs of a passing parade of people and that enjoys the leadership of a long-tenured pastor? Or to create a much smaller congregation that fluctuates in size, vitality, internal harmony or disharmony, outreach, and performance with the quality of the match between that worshiping community and whoever happens to be the current pastor? Or to create a small church in which control is vested in lay volunteers, rather than in the pastor, and ministers can come and go frequently without any long-term impact on the nature of congregational life (except, perhaps, for that occasional extreme mismatch who can produce a sharp decrease in worship

39

ALL RIGHT, PASTOR ALICE, IT'S TIME FOR YOU TO COME OUT and SURRENDER YOUR PULPIT!

Many denominations are uncomfortable with long pastorates!

– FRIAR TUCK

attendance, no matter how small it was before that minister's arrival)?

A second reason for understating the crucial importance of the mission-developer pastor is our inability to be able to identify in advance from among the people on that roster of candidates those who will be highly effective church planters. We do know that neither the quantity of formal education nor the grades received in college or seminary are reliable predictors. We do know that age, race, gender, height, weight, health, place of birth, marital status, and similar measurable characteristics are not reliable predictors.

We do know that level of religious commitment, enthusiasm, productivity, creativity, energy, entrepreneurial skills, persistence, personality, ability to motivate volunteers, vision, future-orientation, zeal, communication skills, patience, competence in raising money, self-reliance, and relational skills are useful predictors, but no one is confident we know how to measure or weigh those characteristics in candidates. We also know that relatively few self-identified "enablers" or "facilitators" have been effective church planters.

Therefore, it is tempting to minimize the role of the mission developer and to focus on those agenda items, such as real estate, subsidies, manuals, surveys, workshops, and communication tools that we are more comfortable in describing and prescribing.

A third explanation for the neglect of this key variable is the widespread discomfort with long pastorates. Some are uncomfortable with "the king and his little kingdom" image that often is communicated by a long pastorate. At least a few believe that both pastor and parish will benefit from changes once every seven to ten years. Others contend it is a free country and therefore a pastor should feel completely free to move to a new challenge whenever the opportunity presents itself.

While this has turned out to be less serious than many had feared, some still are apprehensive about what they are convinced will be an inevitable problem of succession when that long pastorate of twenty-five or thirty or forty years does come to an end. The other side of that issue, of course, is the risk of a major disruption every thirty years or so (and many of these feared disruptions can be avoided) versus a modest disruption every three to five years with the replacement of the current pastor.

A fourth factor is turf. A common example is when either a national staff person or a committee from the regional judicatory has the authority and responsibility for deciding when a new mission will be established, where the permanent meeting place will be located, and the amount of the financial subsidy. The authority for identifying or calling or appointing that mission-developer pastor, however, is vested in a bishop or regional minister or someone responsible for ministerial placement in that regional judicatory. That individual may have accumulated a huge quantity of valuable experience in identifying, screening, and enlisting scores of ministers to organize new churches. Or that individual may have had little or no experience in recruiting church planters in which case it is tempting for everyone concerned to believe the critical decisions are choosing the place, selecting the site, surveying the nearby residents, and raising the money required for initial expenses, and in deciding when that first worship service will be held. It is difficult for those concerned with real estate, finances, and timing to believe those responsibilities are of only minor influence when compared to the potential impact of that decision-making process in selecting that first mission-developer pastor.

Finally, nearly everyone with substantial experience in the organizing of new churches will agree that American Protestantism is faced with a serious shortage of competent church planters. The processes used in identifying and enlisting candidates for the parish ministry in most denominations neither identify nor reward the gifts and skills to be an effective church planter. Few theological seminaries train students in the concepts or skills required to be an effective mission developer. Rarely does that post-seminary apprenticeship, which some contend is a more powerful formative experience than seminary training, nurture the skills and gifts required to be a happy and effective church planter.

Given that shortage of candidates, it is easy to understand why denominational leaders find it tempting to concentrate their energies on variables over which they do have control.

Thus it could be argued that for denominational leaders in general, and especially those responsible for enlisting and training the next generation of pastors, the most critical of these 44 questions is, How do we expand our inventory of qualified church planters? Who will enlist, select, and train the persons who will be church planters? What are the criteria to be used in that selection process?

The Second Variable

The second of these critical variables is vision. What is the vision of those who decided to plant a new congregation in this place? What was in their mind? Were they seeking to plant a new church that eventually would plateau with a couple of hundred members? Or is this envisioned to become a regional church with a thousand or more members? Or was the need to be met to create a non-traditional church to reach people who are repelled by the existing churches here? Or was the perceived need to create an extremely conservative church compared to where other existing congregations fit on that theological spectrum? Or was this vision generated by displaced people (see chapter 10) who moved here and demanded a church of their persuasion? Or was the vision created by members of a long-established congregation who did not want to see their parish grow any larger and who advocated starting a new church as a means of maintaining the status quo in their congregation? Or is the vision a product of the evangelistic imperative of a sponsoring church? Or is it the creation of a dozen or more discontented people who have walked out of a long-established church of this same denomination?

To a substantial degree the vision of what that new mission can and will become creates a self-fulfilling prophecy. This often is reflected in the choice of the person to be the mission developer, the timing, the model chosen for this new venture, the choice of a temporary meeting place, the scheduling and design of that first worship experience, the criteria in the selection of a parcel of land for that first building, the design of the building, decisions on staffing, the priorities in the allocation of the pastor's time, and the assignment of responsibilities to lay volunteers.

In more specific terms that vision for a new church should include a clearly defined and defensible statement of that audience. It should include a carefully formulated methodology for reaching that particular slice of the total population. It should include the ministry goals appropriate to reaching and serving that audience. The vision also should be clear on the style or approach to ministry to be implemented by that mission-developer pastor church planting team. The vision also should be creditable, consistent with the orthodox faith, and motivational.

Those components of the vision should be clearly articulated before the search begins for that church planter. If these are absent from that vision, that places the burden for the strategy on the mission developer. This can mean that the values, dreams, hopes, whims, energy level, marital status, competence, experience, gifts, skills, personality, age, productivity, race, gender, place of birth, education, and goals of the church planter will determine what happens in the process of creating that new congregation. Too often that is the reality despite a veneer of impressive rhetoric. That is the reason the choice of the mission-developer pastor is placed first on this list of the three critical variables. Who chooses that person and what are the criteria for that selection process?

The importance of an inspiring vision explains why leadership is added to this list of critical variables.

The Third Variable

The third of these three critical variables is one many veterans in new church development insist should be first. This is leadership. Under this broad umbrella is the leadership role and style of the church planter. Also under this umbrella are the leadership skills, experience, vision, courage, creativity, and gifts of the denominational executives responsible for creating a strategy of new church development. Rarely can this leadership come from a committee with a rotating membership. Far more often it comes from the person with a decade or two or three of experience in church planting.

Who carries this leadership responsibility in your denomination or regional judicatory? What assets do they bring to this responsibility?

Leaders will be expected to be prepared to respond to most of the questions raised in this book. The first may be whether the top priority in the allocation of scarce resources, including ministerial leadership, should be to planting new churches or to helping long-established congregations grow in numbers. (See chapter 1.) In several denominations another relevant issue may be the choice between starting new churches or "adopting" independent congregations seeking a denominational affiliation. (See chapter 3.) A new question is the possibility of intentionally encouraging the emergence of more multi-site congregations (see chapter 4) rather than concentrating all resources on single-site parishes. Leaders also should be prepared to offer informed advice on the criteria to be used in selecting both a temporary meeting place and a permanent location. (See chapter 5.) In today's world, which is filled with a growing number of very large churches, leaders should be prepared to offer counsel on the four questions on size discussed in chapter 6 and on televangelism as a tool for evangelism (chapter 8) versus direct mail (chapter 9). One of the crucial roles for leaders lies in helping new congregations define their distinctive identity. (See chapter 10.)

The identification, roles, and responsibilities of the leaders rank among the top half-dozen questions to be asked as you prepare your strategy for new church development!

In summary, high quality responses to three questions practically guarantee the success of any venture in new church development today.

1. Who is the church planter?

2. What was the vision behind this venture and was it an influential factor in the selection of that mission-developer pastor?

3. How competent are the leaders who are initiating this venture?

The remaining forty questions in this book are of secondary importance to those three.

CHAPTER THREE

Adoptions and Divisions

For most of American church history nearly every worshiping congregation carried a denominational affiliation. As recently as 1906 only slightly more than one-half of 1 percent of the 194,497 Protestant congregations were classified as "Independent." These 1,079 independent or unaffiliated congregations reported a combined total of 75,000 members or slightly more than one-third of 1 percent of all church members.[1]

Although no one knows the exact number of independent or nondenominational or unaffiliated Protestant churches in existence in 1990, a reasonable estimate is the number exceeds 25,000, and it may be closer to 100,000 if one includes unaffiliated house churches and storefront congregations. Their combined attendance at Sunday morning worship certainly exceeds five million and may be closer to ten million. If they all united to create a new Protestant denomination, a highly unlikely possibility, this not only would be the largest Protestant body in North America, it also would include the greatest diversity of people in terms of the racial, language, and ethnic composition of the membership. It also would cover the full theological spectrum from those to the theological left of the Unitarians to those well to the right of today's fundamentalists. Perhaps the most threatening of its characteristics is that it would be the fastest growing of all Protestant religious bodies on this continent. It would outstrip all other denominations in the pace of new church development, especially in the larger cities.

Do We Adopt?

From a denominational perspective this rapid increase in the number of independent churches raises an interesting policy

46

question. Do we increase the number of congregations in our denomination only by organizing new missions or are we open to other possibilities? For those denominations, like the American Baptist Churches in the U.S.A., who are open to other possibilities, one part of a larger denominational growth strategy could include encouraging independent congregations to affiliate with that denomination.

Why?

Two questions immediately surface when this subject is broached. Why would an inde-

THEY DON'T LOOK LIKE OUR FAMILY, THEY LOOK BETTER!

Adopting growing churches may be one of the best ways of creating new churches!
—FRIAR TUCK.

pendent church want to affiliate with our denomination? Why should we encourage that?

The first question is the easier one to answer since the historical record is clearer and easier to analyze. Nine reasons are articulated repeatedly.

Perhaps the most obvious reason is it can be lonely out there all by yourself. After the excitement of pioneering a church begins to wear off, some of the people begin to regret this isolation from other churches. Paul's repeated emphasis on the interdependence of the churches may cause some to reexamine the reasons for this isolation from other Christian churches. One alternative is to create an informal fellowship with other independent churches. A common outcome of that has been to create a new denomination. A third alternative is to affiliate with an established denomination.

A second reason for seeking affiliation is to gain access to denominational resources such as Christian education materials, staff specialists, guaranteed low interest construction loans, camps, and retreat centers. This has been sufficient to cause congregations to seek "dual affiliation" with a second religious

THEY'VE LOVED ME FOR TEN YEARS BUT WHAT ABOUT TOMORROW?

In a need for security, many a pastor has moved an independent church into a dependable denomination!

—FRIAR TUCK

body. It also should be noted that scores of immigrant congregations seek to affiliate with a North American denomination while retaining their affiliation with the "mother church" in Samoa or Armenia or Korea or the Philippines or Germany or some other country. This pattern traces back through the nineteenth century to colonial days.

For those pastors who have begun to think about retirement, a third reason to affiliate is to be able to be part of a well-managed retirement fund. More recently, a fourth and increasingly attractive reason to be eligible to gain membership in a group health insurance fund.

While it is seldom articulated this crudely, affiliation with a long-established and widely respected denomination can be one step on that ladder of upward mobility.

For that minister who is the second or subsequent pastor in an independent church's history, a powerful reason to affiliate with a large denomination is that this may offer an answer to that question, What happens if they fire me? Most denominations offer assistance to the pastor seeking a new call if that pastor has ministerial standing in that denomination. Occasionally this means the pastor seeks ministerial standing even though the congregation refuses to seek affiliation with that denomination. Sometimes the granting of ministerial standing is sufficient to gain entrance into the pension fund and/or group health insurance.

A seventh reason is the most subjective and difficult to pin down. It is the opposite of why other churches choose to terminate a denominational relationship. As the years roll past and new leaders come into office, some of them begin to raise

48

serious biblical, theological, and ecclesiastical questions about their status. In the case of the independent church, this may result in a study of a half-dozen denominations to determine the one with which they should affiliate. When that has been decided, the congregation votes to knock on that denominational door.

An eighth motivating factor behind an independent church's desire to affiliate with an established denomination is for help in finding a new pastor. This was more common eight to twelve decades ago when a pastor often would accept a call to an unaffiliated congregation only on the condition that church would seek affiliation with the denomination in which that clergyman held ministerial standing. While less common today, it still occasionally is the prime reason.

Nearly every denominational merger results in some congregations deciding to seek another affiliation. One alternative is to create a new denomination. Another is to affiliate with a denomination with a similar tradition, theological stance, and value system.

Finally, some independent churches choose to return home. The reasons behind their decision to secede have evaporated into the past, new leadership is now in office in both the congregation and the regional judicatory, and it is relatively easy to re-affiliate.

When the merger that created the United Church of Christ occurred, several hundred congregations chose either (a) not to become part of the new denomination or (b) not to vote on that issue and to remain outside. A new generation of leaders in these "Schedule I" and "Schedule II" churches today may be open to the merits of a denominational affiliation.

Most of the congregations seeking a denominational affiliation tend to be (a) relatively new and/or (b) composed largely of recent immigrants and/or (c) served by a successor to that original founding pastor and/or (d) African-American and/or (e) located in an urban community where the impact of isolation can be more painful.

Why would any denomination agree to the request of an independent congregation for affiliation? The answers constitute a long list and include (1) an open and inclusive doctrine of the church, (2) an effort to be a good neighbor and to respond

I WONDER HOW YOUR GREAT-GRAND-DADDY NOW FEELS ABOUT WOMEN BECOMING ORDAINED?

Many of the reasons behind past church splits have vanished!

—FRIAR TUCK·

affirmatively on their agenda, not ours, to congregations that seek our help, (3) a desire to broaden the racial, language, ethnic, and social class mix of people and churches in this denomination, (4) a decision to shift from a role as a regional denomination to a self-identified "national church" role, (5) a deep-seated and carefully thought-out belief that "our denomination is a legitimate order of God's creation and we should be open to and welcome all churches that share our doctrinal stance," (6) this can be a cost effective component of a church growth strategy, and (7) Why not?

Perhaps the most serious reservation about adoption is the temptation to make this a critical component of a larger set of institutionally self-serving goals such as to become "an inclusive denomination," or to "reverse our numerical decline of the past two decades," or to be able to brag about "our pluralism." At this point it is easy to justify institutional goals rather than to focus on the needs of the neighbor. Therefore the question to be asked is not, How will our denomination benefit from this new relationship? but rather, Will this new relationship benefit our neighbor?

Should We Colonize?

One of the most frequently articulated questions about new church development has long historical roots. Literally thousands of congregations trace their origins back to when the leaders at another church of that denomination decided to send a "colony" of members out to constitute the nucleus for a new mission.[2]

A common pattern was for the leaders at First Church to

identify the time and place and to take the initiative. Sometimes the mother church purchased land for a future church site and also paid the salary of the minister assigned the responsibility for leading two or three or four dozen families who were commissioned to be the nucleus. Sometimes a group of members got together on their own initiative, found a part-time preacher to lead worship, and met for a year or two before a resident pastor was secured. In hundreds of other cases the initial step was to establish a branch Sunday school as a part of the

WHERE HAVE ALL THE CHILDREN GONE?

Many a mother church has given-up her future establishing new churches!
—FRIAR TUCK

mother church's evangelistic witness. Occasionally the pastor left with a core of volunteers to found that new congregation and the mother church sought a replacement minister. Whatever the details, these ventures usually had the active support of leaders in the mother church.

What happened?

Frequently, this meant a group of younger families composed largely of venturesome, risk-taking, optimistic, pioneering, entrepreneurial, and future-oriented people left the mother church to constitute that nucleus. After sending out two or three of these colonies this often changed the membership mix back at the mother church, which found itself with relatively few younger and venturesome leaders and an excessive proportion of older, past-oriented, cautious, conservative, and unusually prudent leaders. Fifteen years later, the complaint at the mother church was, "We sacrificed all of our best young leadership to help get that new mission started and now we are short of competent leaders." Others regretted that earlier decision with expressions such as, "The reason we don't have young people and our Sunday school is shrinking is because we sent all our best young families out to that mission." While that is less than a complete and accurate diagnosis, it does describe a common result.

A more serious consequence is that colony of people often set out to recreate the mother church, only in an improved and modernized model. Instead of creating a new and different congregation to reach people the mother church could not attract, the new mission competed with the mother church, often from a better location with more attractive facilities, for the same slice of the population that the mother church had been serving. Instead of cloning mother, it might have been better to start a new mission designed to reach and serve people who could not be reached by that sponsoring congregation.

A not uncommon consequence of these two patterns of institutional behavior was that eventually the mother church sold that central city property and merged assets and members with the daughter church at that new site.

A variation in the colonizing pattern traces back to that generous and mission-oriented pastor of old First Church who recruited several of his best leaders to be "loaned" to the new mission for one year after which they would return and resume their leadership role back at First Church. In addition to the tendency to clone, rather than to create a new model to reach a different segment of the population, that model often produced a surprise for that generous pastor. Most of those "members-on-loan" became so excited with the chance to help pioneer a new mission and the opportunity of writing a new rulebook rather than be bound by decades-old traditions back at First Church that they canceled the plan to return. One result was that many of these pastors decided not to do that again.

Another problem that occasionally accompanied the decision to send out a colony to start a new mission came when a generous and well-intentioned member of the mother church offered a gift of a free parcel of land for the meeting place. Too often that gift was eagerly accepted even though it may have been a bad location or a poor site or too small in size. A generation or two later the members regretted the acceptance of that gift.

From a denominational perspective the big advantages of the colonizing approach was that it was and is a simple and low cost way to create additional new churches. Sometimes the mother church not only provided that colony of members, paid the salary of the first pastor for a year or two, and purchased the land, but also made a substantial financial contribution toward the construction of the first building.

Today the concept of sending out colonies of members to start a new mission is widely practiced by independent and nondenominational churches, but many experienced denominational leaders have earned reservations about the merits of this model.

IF YOUR PEOPLE ARE GROWING TIRED of SEEING THE SAME OLD FACES, SUNDAY AFTER SUNDAY...

WATCH THIS SITE GROW A NEW CHURCH

One of history's great lessons: New churches attract new people!
— FRIAR TUCK

A variation of this is the "sponsor church" concept that is a growing practice and will be referred to later. One version is for one or more churches in Ohio to raise the money to pay for the site for a new mission in Florida. Another version is for several sponsoring churches to provide the volunteer crews who will construct that first meeting house for a new mission. Or a sponsor church may agree to (a) pay for the cost of a 50,000-piece direct mailing (see chapter 9) or (b) provide a choir on the first Sunday of every month while another sponsor church provides the choir for the second Sunday, a third for the third Sunday, or (c) a sponsor church pays the salary of one staff member of that new mission for one year or (d) a sponsor church contributes the cost of one room in that new building on condition that within ten years that new mission will contribute the cost of an equivalent room to some other church (this amounts to an interest-free loan for up to ten years that is adjusted for inflation) or (e) the sponsor church makes an interest-free loan for three to five years to help finance the cost of that new building or (f) the sponsor churches contribute annually to a fund for establishing new missions that is administered by a denominational entity. This approach offers many advantages without the disadvantage of sending out a cadre of people to constitute the nucleus for that new mission.

The Walkouts

"Southern Baptists are like amoebas," explained an Associational Director of Missions. "They divide and multiply." This has been the source of literally thousands of new congregations during the past fifteen decades. The typical pattern is for a group of discontented members to walk out and organize a new congregation. One source of this discontent has been the dispute over either the calling or proposed dismissal of the minister. A second has occurred in immigrant churches when a group of second- or third-generation members left to create an English language church. A third reason behind the walkout may have been a doctrinal dispute. A fourth, which was far more common in the nineteenth century than today, was "the lodge question." One faction believed it was impossible for a Christian to be a member of a secret society while others did not believe this produced mutually exclusive loyalties. More recently self-identified charismatic Christians have left a non-charismatic church to create a new Spirit-filled congregation. In a significant minority of cases the resident pastor initiated and led that walkout group.

In some cases the departing members also left that denominational family while on other occasions the walkout produced an additional congregation for that denomination. As a general rule it has been more difficult for discontented Presbyterians and Methodists to walk out and still retain their denominational affiliation. By contrast, it usually has been easier for Baptists, Lutherans, Disciples of Christ, Mennonites, and Reformed Church members to walk out but remain within that denomination.

As a general rule, the stronger the congregational approach to local church government, the easier it is for a group of discontented members to walk out and remain within that denomination. The stronger the connectional ties, the more likely this division will result in the discontented people leaving to join another denomination or to organize an independent church.

A variation on this theme is when the majority of members vote to relocate and use the accumulated assets for construction of a new meetinghouse at a new and larger site. The majority take the name, assets, and historical continuity with them while the minority purchases the real estate, selects a new name, and creates what is legally a new congregation that meets in the old building. Recent examples of this approach to creating new congregations can be found in Chicago, New York, Cleveland, Nashville, Houston, Orlando, and other cities.

WHAT LOOKED LIKE FREEDOM-TO-ROAM REALLY MEANT NOT FAR-FROM-HOME!

Denominational ownership and connectional ties can hinder initiative!
—FRIAR TUCK.

A denominational and/or congregational policy on the possible annexation of independent churches and another policy on encouraging or discouraging the sending out of colonies, either intentionally or unintentionally or as the result of an internal dispute should be considered when developing a strategy for developing new churches.

A growing number of congregations have concluded it is possible to "divide and multiply" by offering the discontented another option, and that raises a seventh question for those interested in new church development.

CHAPTER FOUR

The Multi-Site Option

"At least one-third of our members, including close to a majority of our younger families, want to sell this old property and relocate to a larger site where we could have plenty of off-street parking and construct a new and modern building," explained the troubled pastor. "It is clear to me, however, that most of our members, including nearly all of our long-time members, are opposed to relocation. What should we do? Relocate or stay here in this old building with less than a dozen off-street parking spaces?"

At least a couple hundred churches have responded to that either-or dilemma with a simple one-word decision, "Yes." They have chosen to be multi-site congregations. This usually means that the congregation continues as one legal corporation with one governing board, one staff, one budget, one building fund, and one membership roll, but with two (or more) worship services on Sunday morning, two Sunday schools, and, occasionally, two sets of trustees. It is a way to have one's cake and eat it, too.

On a long-term basis this arrangement usually produces one of four different outcomes. Most commonly these multi-site churches eventually separate, each to become a self-governing congregation. On at least a few occasions this was planned from day one to be a temporary arrangement until a full set of buildings could be constructed at the new site that would include sufficient space to accommodate all the members. In a second group of multi-site experiences this arrangement provided sufficient time for those opposed to relocation to see the new facilities at the new site and gradually talk themselves into supporting the relocation effort. What was publicized as an open-ended arrangement became a transitional stage in a five-to-ten-year relocation process.

A third outcome is to leave it as a completely open-ended

arrangement and trust the leaders of twenty years hence to make wise decisions on the next steps. Few can do that.

A fourth outcome is to design and seek to perpetuate this as a permanent arrangement. The reasons vary tremendously, but among the most common are these.

This can be a means for people to enjoy the spontaneity, intimacy, and warm fellowship that can be achieved in a congregation averaging two hundred to five hundred at worship, which is an impossible goal in the huge parish where anonymity becomes a mixed blessing. At the same time this arrangement enables the members to benefit from the extensive programming, the specialized ministries, the broad-based support of missions and outreach, the range of choices, and the professional staff that requires a big membership base to support it.

For others the number-one advantage is the simplified Sunday morning schedule that consists of Sunday school followed by a fellowship period followed by worship followed by fellowship. Without the pressures to crowd two (or three) worship services and/or two or three sessions of the Sunday school into Sunday morning, it is relatively easy to devise a popular schedule. Those who hold a strong preference for an early schedule can go to one site while those who place a high priority on sleeping late on Sunday morning can go to the other site. The same minister may preach at both locations every Sunday or the arrangement may call for two different preachers or the two ministers may rotate locations and thus prepare a new sermon every other week.

Those who place evangelism and numerical growth at the top of the priority list often support the multi-site concept because it enables one parish to reach and serve a far larger number of people than most congregations can reach from one location.

Others defend it as a means of enhancing the cultural, racial, and ethnic diversity within a congregation as one site is located in a lower-middle class neighborhood and the other site in an upper-middle class neighborhood. In at least a few parishes this arrangement includes four or five sites, thus enabling one congregation to reach and serve residents of the larger community under one institutional umbrella.

While this is something of a means-to-an-end issue, one of the fringe benefits of the multi-site arrangement can be the retention

JOIN OUR CONGREGATION and YOU CAN WORSHIP at THE CHURCH of YOUR CHOICE!

A multi-site arrangement can be a many splendored allurement!

—FRIAR TUCK

for many years of the staff member who would like to (a) preach forty-five Sundays a year, (b) carry few administrative burdens, and (c) concentrate on becoming a highly skilled specialist who can focus his or her energies largely on preaching and on one-program responsibility, such as ministries with families that include teenagers or teaching or missions or social justice or pastoral counseling or young adults or adult Christian education or pastoral visitation. Very few single-site churches can offer a staff position with that combination.

Thus far the multi-site concept has been used most often by Southern Baptists, Presbyterians, Episcopalians, the Christian Church (Disciples of Christ), the Luteran Church-Missouri Synod, and several independent churches. The critical variable is that subsequent senior ministers must be at least as committed to the concept as was the pastor who initiated it. Without that, it probably will become a transitional stage, not a permanent arrangement.

The big second variable appears to be the nature of the assimilation process for new members who join after the multi-site arrangement has been established. If a successful effort is made to assimilate new members into that larger fellowship, they will tend to support continuation of this arrangement. This usually means all new members must be actively involved in the life of that parish at both (or all three or all four) sites. That is difficult!

If the assimilation process is designed to encourage new members to identify with the program and people at one site, it will not be long before the new members (this also applies to new staff) will be asking, "Why don't we terminate this arrangement and become a separate and self-governing congregation?"

Should encouragement of multi-site congregations be a component of your larger strategy for planting new churches?

CHAPTER FIVE

Where Do We Meet?

"Well, I suppose we can't stop you if you're determined to start another new church out here, even if we're already over-churched," conceded the pastor from the Hillside Church. The denominational staff member at that Tuesday morning meeting described in chapter 1 had explained that the decision already had been made to organize a new mission in the east end of that once rural, but now urbanizing county. The purpose of this gathering was to seek advice on timing, location, and other variables. When that became clear, the minister from the Hillside Church changed tactics from categorical opposition to protecting the turf of the Hillside Church. "I hope the site you choose will be at least five or six miles west of us. As I told you earlier, we sure don't want a new mission next door to us."

"That's right," agreed Pastor Paul Schultz, "your lowest priced land will be well to the west of us here. That's where you can still find a large parcel of land for a reasonable price. We already have plenty of churches in this end of the county."

"But if we go five or six miles west, that's well beyond where the residential development is taking place, that will mean we would be at least seven or eight miles west of the belt-line highway that goes around the city, and we would be on the wrong side of the journey-to-work routes. We need a site between where people live and where they work," protested the denominational representative.

"Just be patient," encouraged Pastor Schultz, who clearly wanted to discourage potential competition. "Buy a twenty-acre site in a rural area to the west, wait until more people move out there, and you will be able to sell off fifteen acres to pay for the first building."

That Tuesday morning discussion introduces three more of those 44 questions to be raised about planting new churches. The first, Why? was discussed in chapter 1. Another is, Where should we seek a site for a permanent meeting place? Ahead of that is, What should we use for a temporary meeting place?

That Temporary Meeting Place

Deciding where we will meet can be a revealing indicator of the kind of church we wish to have! —FRIAR TUCK

IT'S INEXPENSIVE AND WE DO GET AN OCCASIONAL VISITOR!

SUNDAY SERVICES 7-9:30

Three of the most commonly used temporary meeting places for new missions are (1) public schools, (2) a building used by another congregation (this is especially common with immigrant churches), and (3) a portable building located at the permanent meeting place.

Many years ago the American Lutheran Church experimented with a plan that called for the denomination to purchase the land, design and begin construction of the first unit of what would be permanent facilities, and call a pastor. Ideally the new building would be completed a few weeks following the arrival of the mission-developer pastor who would enjoy the benefits that go with a permanent meeting place, an office, and a sense of "our turf."

The disadvantages included large initial expenditures for the denomination, the temptation for that new pastor and the charter members to be excessively critical of a design they had not helped create, the comparatively large mortgage payments that faced that fledgling congregation, and, sometimes, an unintentional signal for that new mission to start small and stay small.

Today four of the criteria used in selecting a temporary meeting place are location, cost, availability, and adaptability. In those communities in which the local officials are supportive of the plan, this often means the use of a public school building for two or three or four years. In some communities public school officials place a time limit on this arrangement. As a general rule it rarely is wise to continue in a school for more than three or four years. One risk is the dependence on what usually is a low cost meeting place. A fee of $300 to $400 per week may appear high, but that is less than the cost of constructing and maintaining a modest permanent facility when the payments on the mortgage plus utility and insurance costs may exceed $50,000 or $60,000 annually.

A more serious risk is that potential future members may drift away when they realize the limitations on programming due to those rented facilities. It is difficult to build a strong weekday program in a public school building or a bank or a mortuary or a lodge hall or in the facilities available on Sunday morning from a local college.

One alternative is to rent a vacant retail store for those first several months. This usually has the benefit of high visibility and opportunities to encourage "drop-ins" during shopping hours. If that retail space is in a shopping mall, it may be possible to rent a large room designed for public meetings for Sunday morning and/or one or two other mornings.

A strong argument can be made that the list of criteria should be expanded to begin with the question, Whom are we trying to reach and what is the best temporary meeting place for reaching that segment of the population?

Second on that expanded list of criteria should be, What are our priorities in programming, and what will we need to house that program? Thus a storefront in a shopping mall can be a useful temporary facility if the top priority in programming is pastoral counseling. That also can be a good temporary location if the goal is to focus on attracting mature adults. (Pick a mall that welcomes the early morning mall walkers.) The "power center" shopping strip with a handful of big stores across the street or down the road from the enclosed shopping mall may be a good temporary location if the goal is to reach new homeowners with young children.

If the goal is to concentrate on teenagers and young adults, the best temporary meeting place probably will be a small store in a retail trade area that is near the multiple-screen motion picture theater. The public elementary school usually is a bad choice for a temporary meeting place if the goal is to reach teenagers (who know they no longer belong in an elementary school) or young adults who do not have elementary school age children and may not know the location of that school or to launch what is planned to become a megachurch.

If the goal is to reach teenagers and young adults, the motion picture theater may be the ideal temporary location. It is designed for sight and sound—and that is important if the goal is to reach the sight-sound-sensation generation. It is designed for visual communication and for the use of taped music. The stage can be used for the skit or drama or play that illustrates the central theme of that day's worship experience. In many, but not all theaters the stage will accommodate a small orchestra or band. The screen can be used to project a film or the words to the hymns or the video tape that summarizes what happened during the past seven days in the life of the people pioneering that new mission.

Many of these six- or eight- or twelve-screen theaters have rooms of different sizes. During the first couple of months the new mission may use the smallest theater, but when the crowd grows to a couple of hundred, it is simple to move into the next larger room. These theaters always have an abundance of convenient off-street parking, and most young adults already know how to get there. The theater also lends itself to a Christian education program built on audio-visual resources. The big disadvantage is that corporate worship must be over before the theater's staff begins to pop the popcorn to be sold at the Sunday afternoon matinees.

One of the arguments in favor of the storefront over a school or college auditorium or bank or mortuary or as a supplement to a motion picture theater is weekday programming. Another is seven-day-a-week physical visibility. That physical presence during the week can be a significant factor in attracting and meeting potential future members. A third is the image of a seven-day-a-week presence rather than a Sunday-morning-only presence. If at all possible, it is wiser to locate that weekday facility on the ground level of a retail shopping area rather than on the second or third floor of an office building. The visibility usually is far greater in a retail area than in an office building.

Finally, that temporary meeting place should be one that is supportive of your schedule. As a general rule, people who attend Sunday school first are more likely to "stay for church." If the worship experience is followed by fellowship and Sunday school, the temptation for some may be to fulfill their religious obligation by attending worship, talking with friends for a few minutes, and saying, "I guess we'll skip Sunday school today."

Similarly if the design of the teaching ministry and the schedule calls for a big easy-entry Sunday school class taught by the pastor, the temporary place should be able to accommodate that.

Incidentally, that big adult class taught by the pastor may be the one persuasive argument for scheduling Sunday school after worship. If the pastor is interested in making that a "sermon feedback" class, it should follow worship by a few minutes, not by seven days. That type of class can (1) be an attractive entry point for newcomers, (2) facilitate the "getting acquainted" process with first-time visitors, (3) improve the quality and relevance of the sermons, (4) be supportive of the children's division in the Sunday school by modeling the concept that "everybody here goes to Sunday school," and (5) be an attractive means of introducing adults, who have never attended an adult Sunday school class, to that concept.

That Permanent Location

Back in the romantic 1960s a popular theme among upper-middle-class Anglos declared a truly mission-minded congregation would not waste its money on land and buildings, but would devote all its resources to missions and outreach. Today far greater affirmation is being given in support of the traditional concept of each congregation owning and controlling its own permanent meeting place.[1] Perhaps the big contemporary exception to that generalization is the decision by several score upwardly mobile Korean congregations to rent as long as the landlord church will agree to that arrangement.

While the details of choosing and financing that permanent location are discussed in chapter 13, four other factors that should influence that decision should be taken into consideration in selecting the temporary meeting place.

The most obvious factor is that the location of the temporary meeting place and that permanent site are not unrelated variables. If the vision (see chapter 2) calls for this to be a geographical parish, the temporary meeting place should be in reasonably close proximity to that permanent site.

Second, and perhaps more important, the style of ministry is a critical variable. For example, if the goal of reaching the sight-sound-sensation generation leads to the choice of a motion picture theater as the temporary Sunday morning meeting place, the permanent site should be compatible with the goal of reaching that same generation. This means easy access by automobile.

Third, if the vision calls for creating what eventually will become a megachurch, that permanent site should be in a location and of a size (thirty to three hundred acres) that is compatible with that vision. The use of a motion picture theater usually is more compatible with that goal than an elementary school. A high school or community college building usually will be more compatible than the choice of an elementary school. The community college (or high school or university) temporary meeting place helps communicate the image of a regional church while the elementary school tends to convey the image that this is a neighborhood church.

Finally, the combination of "having our own place" plus accumulating equity means that it may be appropriate to purchase an existing religious facility or commercial building or warehouse as a temporary meeting place. This has several advantages in terms of schedule and image and may be a means of accumulating capital toward the construction of that dreamed-of permanent meetinghouse.

In many communities a congregation organized two or three decades ago has decided to relocate to a much larger site in order to achieve the new goal of becoming a megachurch. This may create the availability of an excellent building at a choice location on a three-to-ten-acre parcel of land. That could become an excellent temporary meeting place. If the vision for this new mission calls for it to become a congregation averaging 150 to 700 at worship, this could become an attractive permanent site. The choice of a temporary meeting place could turn into a permanent location for this new mission. That possibility opens up the multifaceted question on size.

CHAPTER SIX

How Large?

Four of the biggest challenges in planting new churches are related to size. One is how many people should we plan to welcome to our first worship service? A second is how many people should we have on that initial staff? A third is how much land will we need for a permanent meeting place? The fourth is how large will our parish be in geographical terms?

The answers to these four questions have much in common. First, the answer given to any of these three will influence the response to the fourth. Second, each can become a self-fulfilling prophecy. Third, and most important, the central factor in determining the answer to each question will be the vision, competence, and commitment of those responsible for planting that new congregation. Less influential will be economic or demographic or regional or denominational or historical considerations. Finally, in most new missions succeeding generations of members will live with the consequences of the answers to those four questions.

Small Groups or Large Crowd?

While scores of exceptions do exist, one of the most effective means yet discovered of planting a new church that eventually levels off with an average worship attendance of a hundred or less is to begin with an initial nucleus of three dozen or fewer people. The size of the crowd on that first Sunday usually (1) indicates to those present the size of this new mission, (2) attracts those who prefer a congregation of that size and repels those who prefer a much larger or much smaller church, (3) begins to suggest the style of interpersonal relationships that will be followed here, and (4) provides that small cadre of leaders with the bench mark for measuring performance—if forty were expected and sixty

attend, that is a success while if two hundred were expected and only a hundred appear, that is a defeat. Thus if one hundred is regarded as a big number, people will tend to be delighted with an attendance of one hundred and ten. If one hundred is perceived as a small number, everyone will agree we have to improve on what we are doing when attendance is one hundred and ten.

Even more influential from a long-term perspective are two other factors. First, the decision to begin small will reinforce one approach to ministry by the church planter or mission developer and that initial cadre of leaders. Likewise the decision to begin large will force the pastor and the other leaders to develop an approach to ministry that is consistent with a large number of people.

The simplest illustration of this decision to begin small is that consistent with the approach to ministry of the pastor who prefers to concentrate on one-to-one relationships with individuals and who conceptualizes this as a collection of eighty people. By contrast, the decision to begin large is consistent with the approach to ministry of the pastor who is a superb preacher, is an excellent teacher, is competent in building the organizational life of the parish, is comfortable delegating responsibilities to others, and conceptualizes this church as a collection of classes, groups, choirs, committees, cells, circles, families, programs, events, and individuals.[1]

IT'S SO SMALL BECAUSE ITS TAP-ROOT WAS SEVERED IN THE BEGINNING!

—FRIAR TUCK

Starting too soon can determine our destiny more than our demographics!

A second facet of this distinction relates to the organizational structure. The decision to begin small is consistent with the desire to minimize the organizational structure, place nearly all the policy making and planning responsibilities in one board, keep the number of committees and meetings to a minimum, and depend largely on that informal grapevine to be the heart of the internal communication system.

The decision to begin large with a goal of building a large congregation is consistent with a willingness to create a more complex organizational structure that includes a policy-making governing board, a set of program committees (Christian education, missions, evangelism, special events, fellowship), two or three administrative committees (finance, real estate), an occasional ad hoc committee, and a one-sheet weekly newsletter that is reinforced by announcements in the bulletin, posters, telephone calls, postcards, special mailings, stories in the local newspaper, that informal grapevine, and video tapes.

Starting small often creates one form of a self-fulfilling cycle of performance while starting large usually sends that new mission down the road to a radically different approach to ministry that in retrospect appears to have been a self-fulfilling prophecy.

Finally, another facet of this question is a product of the fact that internal barriers to numerical growth often are related to size. Only a tiny fraction of Protestant congregations on the

ON THE COUNT OF THREE HUNDRED, WE'LL BREAK INTO ACTION!

In the long run, a team of two to seven people may be the most effective means of starting a new church!

—FRIAR TUCK.

North American continent that have been averaging fewer than a hundred people at worship find it possible to grow substantially in size, regardless of the demographic context. Even more common is the pattern reflected by the thousands of congregations that have remained on a plateau of averaging fewer than thirty-five to forty at worship. Likewise most congregations that do reach an average attendance at Sunday morning worship of 145 to 175 find it difficult to grow up beyond that widely discussed "two hundred barrier."[2]

Thus one of the most persuasive arguments for beginning with at least a couple hundred people at that first worship service is to avoid being trapped in that small church syndrome. This also is the best means of (a) helping newcomers who have no previous church background from feeling conspicuous or like aliens, (b) minimizing the long-term influence of that cadre of charter members, (c) avoiding overload and "burnout" among this initial cadre of volunteers, (d) persuading first-time visitors that is a vital, attractive, lively, exciting, effective, and challenging new ministry, (e) minimizing the need for long-term financial subsidies, (f) mobilizing the resources necessary to offer a full scale program, (g) encouraging a long-tenured pastorate for that first minister and thus avoiding the disruption that often accompanies the premature departure of the founding pastor, (h) reaching the generations of people, both churched and unchurched, born after 1945, (i) avoiding that temptation to function as a small fellowship built around a network of one-to-one relationships with the pastor at the hub of this network that often makes it easy to drift into an unintentional exclusionary stance, (j) encouraging a "large church" approach to ministry that is designed to provide a variety of entry points for future newcomers, (k) helping policy makers see, feel, and understand the need for sufficient space for this new congregation, and (l) making it possible to include competent specialists on the program staff.

Although it is easier to begin with a couple dozen enthusiastic pioneers who enjoy being together, it may be wiser to plan that (a) the first worship service will exceed two hundred people and (b) the attendance will not drop below two hundred during that first formative year. This may mean an attendance of three or four or five hundred on that first Sunday.

How many people do you expect for that first worship service? Fifty? Two hundred? Five hundred? That may be the most influential decision you will make in planting a new church!

Staffing the New Mission

Overlapping that question on the size of the crowd for that first service is the question of staffing that new mission. From a long-term perspective perhaps the most expensive alternative is to staff the new mission with a pastor who is the part-time (or nearly full-time) pastor of another congregation meeting in a building several miles away. This was a widely used system in nineteenth-century American Methodism and turned out to be a (a) very low cost system in terms of the initial investment, (b) means of creating thousands of small congregations, (c) system for planting scores of new missions or preaching points that never reached their tenth birthday, and (d) design that also

TODAY...WILL I BE A CHURCH-PLANTER-EVANGELIST-PIONEER, OR A PASTOR-PREACHER-TEACHER-ADMINISTRATOR?

Many a new mission fails when a lonely planter struggles with a multiplicity of roles!
—FRIAR TUCK ☺

created many vigorous congregations that began to thrive and grow when they received their first full-time resident pastor.

This approach to staffing also was followed in the 1950s and produced a large number of new congregations that plateaued in size with an average attendance of fewer than one hundred.

By far the most common approach in recent decades has been to send a mission developer or church planter out to create that new congregation. Some have produced unbelievable results. Others have walked away in frustration after a year or two or three. Many have enjoyed the experience of building a new congregation that reached an average attendance of one hundred and fifty or more before leveling off in size. Others have succeeded in building a comparatively large congregation within a few years—and seen that new mission shrink drastically shortly after that magnetic first mission developer left and was followed by a minister who turned out, in retrospect, to have been a disastrous mismatch with that congregation. To some it appeared that the continuity was in the personality of that attractive church planter, not in the new congregation.

A widely followed design has been for the mission developer to come on the scene, complete several thousand calls, perhaps make hundreds of telephone calls, send out large volumes of direct mail, and, after four to six months, schedule that first worship service. Four or five months later a full scale program had emerged with regularly scheduled corporate worship, Sunday school, a budget, a women's organization, one or two adult Bible study groups meeting weekly, perhaps a radio program, a youth group, and at least a minimum organizational structure to enable this to become a self-governing and self-financing ministry.

The standard price tag on this sequence is the church planter spends several months as an evangelist identifying potential future members who will help pioneer creation of a new worshiping community. Within several weeks following that first worship service, the minister's role is gradually transformed from church-planter-evangelist-pioneer into pastor-preacher-teacher-organizer-administrator-and-attender of committee meetings. Those ministers who

Yielding to the pressure to begin before we're ready has grounded many a new mission!

are unusually productive workers, who are highly skilled in managing their time, and who display a strong goal orientation often are able to fill both roles effectively until that new mission averages three or four hundred at worship.

For the majority of church planters, however, the second role soon begins to use up all available time and the new mission plateaus at around a hundred or less at worship.

That syndrome has caused many specialists in church planting to conclude that the most effective, and frequently in the long run the lowest cost approach, is to begin with a team of two to seven people.

For many the most persuasive argument for beginning with a team of at least two persons is in response to the date for that first worship service. If one person is assigned to plant a new church, and if the goal is to begin with at least two hundred worshipers, that may mean the first worship service will not be scheduled until six to fifteen months after the arrival of the mission developer. That may be unacceptable to (a) those who initiated this effort to plant a new church and who want immediate and highly visible results, (b) the mission developer who wants to lead worship and

71

preach as soon as possible, and (c) that initial core of potential charter members.

As was pointed out earlier, if the mission developer yields to those pressures to begin corporate worship soon after arrival, that often means (a) beginning with a smaller number and (b) diverting much of that church planter's time and energy away from cultivating new constituents and spending that time on sermon preparation, leading worship, teaching, administration, real estate concerns, and responding to needs for pastoral care. The minister who enjoys preaching and pastoral work will find it easy to succumb to these pressures and to postpone until "next week" the cultivation of prospective new members and perfecting the design for a distinctive personality for that new mission.

One compromise solution is to recruit a team consisting of a pastor and evangelist or parish visitor. The pastor schedules that first worship service a couple of months after arrival and concentrates considerable time on that first service. As the pastor becomes increasingly involved in congregational responsibilities, the evangelist or parish visitor continues on a full-time basis the work of identifying, contacting, and enlisting an ever larger constituency.

One of the often cited advantages of the two-person team is that it is cheaper. This naturally has tremendous appeal to the leaders of smaller denominations and of evangelistic associations that cannot afford a $300,000 to $500,00 subsidy for each new mission. It has less attraction for leaders of the wealthier denominations that endorse and can afford the concept of large subsidies for several years for new missions.

Instead of providing a large outside subsidy over three to six years, the larger initial investment can produce a financially self-supporting congregation in ten to twenty months. This often is accompanied by the expectation that the members of this new congregation will finance the costs of purchasing land and constructing a meetinghouse. The critical variable in this model, of course, is the selection of two adults who (a) can work together as a team and (b) are competent, creative, and productive workers.

Experience suggests it usually is much easier to build a compatible team of three, rather than of two, so a parallel model calls for a three-person team. One is the pastor-preacher-administrator. A second is the evangelist, and the third is a specialist in creating and nurturing small Bible study-mutual support groups. Occasionally the evangelist or the small group specialist, rather than the pastor, accepts the central responsibility for planning each worship experience. Normally, however, the pastor is the team leader, the preacher, and an ordained minister. The other two team members may or may not be ordained ministers. In terms of the total subsidy required for new church development, this may be the lowest cost model.

While the content of the vision behind this new mission may prohibit this, it often is more effective if one member of that team is skilled in building a multi-faceted ministry around music, both instrumental and vocal, drama, and large group events. This can be a critical factor if the goal is to create a new megachurch and/or to reach the sight-sound-sensation generation and/or to make the best use of a motion picture theater as the temporary meeting place.

In several cases none of the three drew a salary for the first several months to a year and were supported by an employed spouse. This variation arouses all kinds of comments about the advantages and disadvantages of subsidies, exploitation, polity, minimum salaries, and the nature of the call to ministry that cannot be discussed here.

If that initial staff consists of five to seven full-time and/or part-time members, it may include a specialist in ministries with families that include young children, another in public relations, one in music, and one in Christian education or ministries with young adults. While exceptions always exist, the basic pattern tends to be the larger the staff (a) the bigger the crowd at that first service, (b) the earlier the new mission becomes self-supporting, (c) the smaller the total subsidy (exclusive of subsidies from employed spouses), and (d) the younger the median age of the membership eighteen months later.

If the goal is to reach African-American parents who have strong upwardly mobile ambitions for their children and/or working class Anglos in the central city, the new mission may be organized around a Christian day school. That, of course, usually requires at least three full-time staff members including the pastor and may require four or five people on that initial team.

How Much Land?

WHEN IT COMES
TO STARTING
A CHURCH,
WE CAN'T HAVE
TOO MANY PLAYERS!

NEW CHURCH
MISSION

A team of three-to-seven is our best guarantee against second Sunday let-downs!

— FRIAR TUCK.

The answer given to any one of these four questions on size has obvious implications for the other three. This becomes clear when the focus is shifted to the amount of land required for a new mission.

Four guidelines will illustrate the complexity of this question. First, a new mission probably will need at least twice as much land as those planning it believe will be necessary. Second, a reasonable goal is a minimum of at least one acre for every one hundred people at worship. Thus if it is assumed this new mission eventually will grow to include a combined total of 2,500 worshipers at three services, that means a minimum of twenty to twenty-five acres.

Third, the younger the members, the more land needed for parking. Thus the two-generation household of five members may require only two parking spaces on Sunday morning. By contrast, four parking spaces will be needed for every five young single adults who come to worship.

Fourth, a reasonable goal is to provide twice the number of off-street parking spaces required by municipal land use regulations.

In a few denominations the primary responsibility for early purchase of what eventually will be the starting places for future churches has been allocated either to a national agency of that religious body or to a private real estate firm. That usually means (a) lower costs, (b) a wider choice of sites, (c) larger sites, and (d) an opportunity to create a self-financing revolving fund that purchases additional sites from the sale of surplus land acquired many years earlier.

Other religious bodies have displayed a preference for a

shorter time frame and/or local control. This may limit the length of the list of attractive sites and result in higher costs per acre. That usually means either larger subsidies to the new mission for capital expenditures or beginning with a team of three rather than a solo church planter.

Perhaps the lesson that has been learned and is frequently cited is that it is relatively easy to find a buyer for the surplus land if that initial site turns out to be too large, but it may be difficult to expand a site that is too small.

The other frequently articulated lesson is that it is wiser to choose a site that will fit tomorrow's circumstances rather than one that would have been ideal for yesterday.

What Is Our Parish?

John Wesley exclaimed, "The world is my parish!" Many of his followers, as well as those who came after Martin Luther, John Calvin, and other reformers, found it more comfortable to think in terms of a relatively small geographical parish. For several generations it was assumed that people either would walk to church or be transported by a horse.

Many decades later Henry Ford, with his populist dream that every family should be able to own an automobile, began to undercut the notion of the geographical parish, but it continued into the 1950s. Even though a rapidly growing proportion of churchgoers went to church via an automobile, it was widely assumed they should walk. That assumption undergirded much of the planning for the new churches founded in the 1950s and even, to a limited extent, the 1960s.

Next came President Dwight D. Eisenhower who pointed to the dream of an interstate highway system as the number-one accomplishment of his eight years in office and the geographical parish was pushed another step toward obsolescence. By the mid-1960s it was widely but not universally recognized that church shoppers placed geographical proximity fairly low on the list of factors in choosing a church. By the late 1970s this low priority given to geographical proximity was obvious in the churchgoing patterns of adults born after 1945, charismatic Christians, retirees, African-Americans, immigrants from the

THE YOUNGER OUR MEMBERS THE MORE ROOM WE'LL NEED FOR PARKING!

Four parking spaces will often be needed for every five single adults!

—FRIAR TUCK

Pacific Rim, an increasing number of Roman Catholics, people on a self-identified religious pilgrimage, young single adults, people in their second or subsequent marriage, theologically conservative Christians, adults with an exceptionally strong denominational affiliation, people of all ages seeking outstanding preaching, those looking for a strong weekday program, theologically liberal Christians, immigrants from Cuba and Puerto Rico, two-career couples, and new converts to the faith.

This obsolescence of the geographical parish represents, along with the preference for a larger site, beginning with a big crowd, and recruiting a team rather than an individual to plant a new mission, four of the radical changes in new church development since 1955.

Instead of expecting to build a constituency for that new church from among people who live within a mile or two of the meeting place, the more effective approach today is to (1) conceptualize the "service area" as a five or ten or twenty or thirty or forty-mile radius, (2) expect to attract not 5 or 10 or 15 percent of the residents of that service area, but perhaps one-tenth or one-half of 1 percent, (3) most important, develop a distinctive approach to ministry, designed to reach one slice of the population, rather than attempting to be able to be all things to all people in one neighborhood.

This change in the geographical definition of "parish" raises three other questions that deserve a new chapter.

CHAPTER SEVEN

Who, Why, and How?

Who are the people we expect to be the first three hundred adult members of this new mission, why would they join us in pioneering a new worshiping community here, and how will we reach them?

That long sentence articulates three of the critical questions facing every church planter or mission developer.

The concept of the homogeneous unit principle has sparked more controversy than any other theory to emerge out of the church movement.[1] In essence this principle declares that most congregations tend to attract new members who closely resemble the people who constitute the current membership. Birds of a feather flock together. The congregation composed largely of never-married adults born after 1960 will tend to attract young single adults. As the years roll by, and most of the members marry and begin to have children, that congregation will begin to exert a stronger appeal to couples with young children. One explanation is most congregations program to serve their current membership; thus the program priorities tend to attract people who resemble the present membership. It also is worth noting that the majority of all people do socialize largely with people from their own age cohort. Only kinship ties, national origins, language, race, specialized programming, denominational ties, social class, the personality and religious views of the pastor, friendship ties, and theological perspective are more powerful forces than the homogeneous unit principle in determining why church shoppers choose a particular congregation, and it can be argued those are all expressions of the homogeneous unit principle.

The homogeneous unit principle should not be ignored by those planning to start new churches! Among the many implications, it suggests that the first hundred members will have a tremendous influence in determining who the next three hundred members will be. Thus a critical decision is the enlistment of that initial cadre of charter members.

Eight Approaches

The easiest course of action is to seek to build a new congregation out of churchgoing Christians with that same denomination affiliation. This was a widely used methodology back in the 1950s when thousands of new churches were organized to "serve our people who have moved out here." In many cases a crew of volunteers surveyed the residents and asked, "Would you be interested in joining a new Presbyterian (or Lutheran or Methodist or Episcopal or Congregational or Baptist) church if one were started out here?" Obviously this alternative had more appeal back when denominational loyalties were stronger and when the target population was drawn largely from among people born in the 1910–30 era, the most churchgoing generation in American history.

Today this approach is still followed by those who prefer to build small congregations. Sometimes that emphasis on creating small new missions is reinforced by (a) choosing an elementary school as the temporary meeting place, (b) selecting as the mission developer a minister who has never served a large church, and (c) providing long-term financial subsidies.

A second alternative surfaced under the label of "community church." The word "Community" replaced "First," "St. Paul," and "Trinity" or a street name as the most popular name for a new mission. In part, that was a recognition of the dwindling appeal of a denominational brand name to younger adults, in part a reaction against denominational categories, in part a result of the desire by mission developers to reach beyond their own denominational family, in part a product of the emergence of thousands of new "independent" or "nondenominational" or "transdenominational" congregations and in part a result of that intentional effort by several nondenominational seminaries and Bible colleges to enlist and train people to see church planting as their special calling.

An earlier force that is of less significance today was the naive hope that a new mission carrying the word "Community" in its name could reach a far larger proportion of the nearby residents, many of whom had dropped out of a denominationally related church, than could the new mission that flew the denominational flag. Today the power of that word "Community" to attract a flood of new members is largely in the heads of the people who select the name for a new mission. Frequently it is chosen to avoid use of a denominational identification that may communicate more or less than is intended. Perhaps the strongest argument in support of the choice of that word as a name is that in various

GULP! I SURE HOPE IT LANDS SOMEWHERE SOFT!

Few new missions can hope to meet more than two or three unmet needs!
— FRIAR TUCK

places on the continent such words as "Lutheran" or "Episcopal" or "Brethren" or "Baptist" or "Anglican" or "Presbyterian" or "Church of Christ" or "Unitarian" are perceived to be exclusionary terms.

3   A third alternative in determining the identity of those first few hundred members of a new mission is to adopt and implement the slogan, "Find a need and meet it!"

This can be an exceptionally effective approach, depending in part on the creativity, openness, and skill of the church planter, but for obvious reasons it also represents a decision to follow the homogeneous unit principle. Only a tiny fraction of all new missions have the resources required to respond to more than two or three distinctive unmet needs, thus most of those first hundred members will have much in common.

Perhaps the most common example of this alternative is to begin with a strong Bible teaching focus in an effort to reach adults who are seeking that type of ministry. This often attracts people on a serious religious pilgrimage, churchgoers who are dissatisfied with the current pastor of the church to which they belong, people born and reared in a Roman Catholic family, adults born after 1945, church shoppers who have just moved to that community, malcontents, lonely adults, and those reared in a liberal Protestant tradition.

Another example is to create a "spirit-filled" new mission carrying the label of a mainline Protestant denomination. This represents an effort to build on denominational loyalties, the power of the Holy Spirit, and the desire to reach out and serve others in the name of Christ.[2]

A parallel thrust that accounts for much of the recent growth of the Assemblies of God and several other religious bodies is to offer a response to those who are searching for an experiential, rather than an intellectual and rational, approach to the Christian faith.[3] This often attracts large numbers of well-educated adults.

Other examples include new missions organized around a strong emphasis on recreation or on serving families that include a developmentally disabled member or on attracting gays and lesbians. In other new missions the central appeal is participatory worship or a Christian day school or ministries with families that include young children or travel and study or serving self-identified charismatic Christians who retain a powerful denominational loyalty or on a place to meet and make new friends or a well-organized and high quality Sunday school that causes children to look forward eagerly to returning the following Sunday or a weekday early childhood development center or on growth groups[4] or an after-school ministry with elementary age youngsters and their parents or a desire to reach the "sight-sound-sensation" generation.

In recent years the most highly visible and widely copied approach to identifying those initial members has been to concentrate on identifying, reaching, attracting, and serving unchurched adults. This includes both those who once were active churchgoers and self-identified Christians as well as those who never were actively involved in the life of any worshiping community. This focus on the unchurched requires a radically different style of ministry than is utilized by those new church developers who are seeking to "reach our people who are moving out here."

During the 1980s most of the new missions that were effective in reaching unchurched adults and/or adults on a religious pilgrimage were not affiliated with any of the traditional mainline Protestant denominations on this continent. Their success explains part of the numerical decline in hundreds of long-established Presbyterian, Methodist, Lutheran, Baptist, Disciples of Christ, United Church of Christ, Brethren, Episcopal, and Roman Catholic congregations.

Innovation in preaching and worship isn't encouraged by many denominations!
—FRIAR TUCK

Successful attempts to reach those who are not actively involved in the life of any worshiping community often involve a non-traditional form of worship, a greater emphasis on music, more special events and meaningful experiences, and a different approach to preaching. It may be difficult for the pastor, who has spent years learning, practicing, and perfecting traditional approaches to ministry, to adopt and implement a radically different style. For example, in several of the very large congregations composed largely of people born after 1955 the sermon is thirty-five to fifty minutes long, not the widely recommended twelve to twenty minutes, and includes memorable paragraphs of instruction in the faith. It may be even more difficult to secure the approval from one's ministerial colleagues and from denominational leaders for that new approach. If it works, and that style often does produce a large and rapidly growing new mission, it may be simply unrealistic for a pastor to expect affirmation from his or her peers. That helps explain why so few of the relatively new megachurches of today are related to any denomination and especially to those created before 1860.

A fifth approach, which has been described earlier and is now largely a part of the past, is to clone the mother church. The sending out of a nucleus of fifty to five hundred people to form the sponsoring congregation usually means that future new

THAT'S MY BOY! (HONEST!)

Successful new churches are seldom clones of existing churches!

—FRIAR TUCK.

members will closely resemble the people who constitute that initial nucleus.

Perhaps the most frustration-producing facet of this methodology can be seen when the sponsoring church traces its origins back to a successful attempt to reach and serve adults without any active church relationship. Fifteen years later this thriving, vital, and evangelistic congregation feels compelled to sponsor a new church to reach the unchurched in another community.

What happens? The sponsoring church does not send out unchurched adults as a nucleus! That initial cadre consists of people who are committed Christians, dedicated churchgoers, and firm believers. Frequently their appeal turns out to be to members of other churches who are discontented with the congregation of which they are a part and who are open to a message that speaks to their personal needs. In other words, that nucleus, most of whom see themselves on a religious pilgrimage, go out and found a new mission. They do not design it to reach unchurched adults. They design it to meet the religious needs of pilgrims on a faith journey similar to their own. Thus their strongest appeal often is to other churchgoing Christians on a faith journey. Advocates of the homogeneous unit principle observe this phenomenon and comment, "Naturally." Meanwhile, the complacent, contented, serene, and self-satisfied unchurched adults ignore that new mission and read the newspaper or go jogging on Sunday morning.

It is difficult to overemphasize the tendency for the characteristics of the people who constitute that initial nucleus to be remarkably influential in determining the identity of the next few hundred new members.

A sixth, and far and away the most common approach to

identifying who the first couple hundred new members will be, occurs in the process utilized in the selection of the mission-developer pastor. Nearly all of the new members of that new congregation will be people who are attracted by the personality, style, priorities, theological perspective, value system, energy, vision, world view, and other characteristics of that church planter. Obvious illustrations of this pattern include (a) the mission developer who came to this continent from Korea a few years ago who probably will create a new congregation composed largely of adults who were born in Korea, (b) the mission developer who is a self-identified charismatic Christian who probably will build a new congregation composed largely of charismatic Christians, (c) the African-American mission developer who probably will organize a new church composed largely of people who can trace at least part of their ancestry back to natives of Africa or the Caribbean, (d) the bilingual mission developer born in Cuba who probably will attract many new members who also trace their ancestry back to Cuba, (e) the theologically liberal pastor who probably will

LIKE IT OR NOT, THE NUCLEUS ALWAYS CLONES ITS OWN!

Our first hundred members will attract others with those same needs!
—FRIAR TUCK.

HMM-M! A COUPLE of PIGEONS... ERR...I MEAN GOD-LOVED SPARROWS!

Positive homogeneity becomes a reality when those once unchurched reach out to the currently unchurched!
—FRIAR TUCK.

WOW! ANOTHER FAN WANTS TO BECOME A MEMBER!

Nearly all new members of a new mission are attracted by the personality of the church planter!

— FRIAR TUCK.

enlist as new members people who share a liberal, rational, and intellectual approach to the faith, (f) the mission developer who spent thirty years serving small congregations who probably will attract those who prefer a small church and the new mission will plateau in size before the average attendance at worship reaches 135, and (g) the mission developer who never graduated from high school and who probably will draw many adults who never finished the twelfth grade.

This point is reinforced by those specialists in new church development who can recall the 1960s when the slogan was, "The three critical factors in launching a new church are location, location, and location." Today many of these veterans substitute the word "pastor" three times for the word "location."

A seventh factor in determining who the first couple hundred members will be is the nature and location of that temporary meeting place. As is pointed out in chapters 5 and 13, that choice of a temporary meeting place will send out many messages about who is expected. This probably ranks among the top three or four variables in determining both who will constitute the first few hundred members and in influencing the growth curve of that new mission.

Finally, the most obvious factor in determining the identity of those first few hundred members is the process used to invite people to attend. Whom do we invite is a critical question and the answer often creates a self-fulfilling prophecy.

Why Will They Come Here?

Perhaps the most elusive and subjective issue raised in this book is, Why would anyone join this new mission? This also is an urgent question for leaders in middle and upper middle income Anglo denominations, determined to launch new missions in inner-city African-American neighborhoods or in public housing projects or in low income Anglo communities.

In white suburban communities one common response can be summarized under the umbrella of "the law of averages." In more precise terms this is based on the experiences of scores of suburban mission developers who explain that if they complete personal visits in a thousand homes, they can expect to enlist fifteen to twen-

... JOHN SMITH PARTS HIS HAIR in THE MIDDLE, JACK SMYTHE HAS A CREW-CUT and JON SCHMIDT HAS NO HAIR AT ALL!

A friendly pastor who can remember names is an asset!

— FRIAR TUCK©

ty adults who will respond favorably to the challenge to help pioneer a new church. Some of the highly energetic pastors with an unusually attractive personality who also are highly skilled in making this type of evangelistic call report their success rate is closer to 3 or 4 percent. This is more likely to be true if the area includes a relatively large proportion of (a) upwardly mobile displaced people who moved here recently because of a job, (b) young parents reared in the Roman Catholic Church, (c) adults who are half of an interfaith or interdenominational marriage, (d) persons who are substantially higher on the social class scale than their parents and display upwardly mobile ambitions for their children, (e) two-career couples, (f) successful entrepreneurs, (g) long-established Protestant congregations that display a strong member orientation, (h) retired couples who have moved at least thirty miles from their previous place of residence since retirement, and/or (i) adults born after 1955 who grew up in a theologically liberal congregation.

In recent years, as door-to-door visitation has produced more frustrations and fewer results, this law of averages concept has been expanded to place greater reliance on direct mail, newspaper advertisements, radio, television, telemarketing (see chapter 8), and other channels of communication. This also has lowered the response rate. Instead of the 1 or 2 percent rate achieved in door-to-door visitation, these channels of communication are more likely to produce a one-tenth or one-twentieth of 1 percent rate of positive responses.

In all cases the response to this question, Why will they come? is, "Because we invited them." The law of averages approach can be translated, "We invite everyone and begin with those who respond."

If that initial invitation is delivered in person by the mission-developer pastor making a twenty- to sixty-minute visit, the vast majority of those who appear for that first worship service will become charter members. If those first-time visitors appear in response to an ad in the newspaper or a telephone call or a piece of direct mail publicity, a much smaller proportion will return on the second and succeeding Sundays and will become charter members.

Here again it is difficult to overemphasize the influence of the pastor's personality, style of ministry, enthusiasm, vision, ability to call people correctly by name, productivity, preaching, and leadership ability. Only a small fraction of church planters are able to send complete strangers home from the first meeting filled with enthusiasm and eager to return.

A radically different response to this, Why will they come? question is when the message is changed from a general invitation to a specific promise. One example is the letter that articulates a half dozen of the most common questions raised by laypeople about the Christian faith and promises these will be answered in the first six sermons. Another letter may ask, Are you looking for a Sunday school with caring teachers for your children? Another is an invitation to help pioneer a Tuesday evening Bible study class. Another pastor may invite those "who are seeking a church that does not offer rote answers to complex questions, but is designed for the thinking person with serious questions." A different church planter invites those who want to be part of "a spirit-filled church."

One of the most attractive invitations for the 1990s is the one that promises "we are a family-centered congregation prepared to strengthen family life."[5] A growing number of parents, especially single-parent mothers, are seeking a church that can deliver on that promise. A crucial distinction is between rhetoric and performance. The new mission may be able to deliver on the promise to affirm traditional family values, but few new churches have the resources (physical facilities, specialized staff, money, creativity, and commitment) to offer a strong family-centered program. This promise usually requires beginning with a staff of three to five people, two of whom are extremely compe-

tent in translating family-systems theory into program.

A third explanation for why people come was more widespread in the 1950s than today. It is based on the assumption people will come to a new mission because of geographical proximity and/or denominational loyalties and/or a sense of obligation and/or "because it will be a good place for your children."

While it is chosen by a relatively small proportion of new missions, another answer to that question of why will they come is to focus on church shoppers. The new missions designed to appeal to church shoppers usually will display at least a half dozen of these common characteristics: (a) an easy-to-find and attractive meeting place with a surplus of convenient off-street parking, (b) outstanding, memorable, persuasive, credible, well-organized, relevant, and biblically based sermons that capture and hold the attention of that first-time visitor and motivate that person to return, (c) a beginning date for that first service in April or early May, just ahead of the peak church shopping season that in most places runs from mid-May to late September, (d) a well-organized children's Sunday school staffed with loving and skilled teachers (some of whom may be on loan for a couple of months from a

Speech: I'D MISS MY VACATION FOR THEM!

COMING ATTRACTIONS
ADULT STUDY OPTIONS
CHILD CARE PROVIDED

WORSHIP SERVICES EVERY 1½ HOURS

POPCORN

Building toward that first worship service is as important as building that first building!

—FRIAR TUCK

sponsoring church), (e) an attractive, easy-to-find and clean nursery staffed by at least one mature adult, (f) an exciting and easy-to-follow worship format with familiar hymns for congregational singing, (g) a good choir (which also may be borrowed from the sponsoring church), (h) a cadre of friendly, smiling, and well-trained greeters who aggressively seek out and welcome every visitor, (i) a gregarious, extroverted, and friendly minister who also excels in remembering people's names, (j) an easy-to-reach and staffed refreshment-information table that is located between the place of worship and the major exit from that temporary meeting place, (k) a carefully designed and redundant system for identifying first-time visitors and obtaining their name, address, and other data, (l) a cadre of trained visitors, usually led by the minister, who will call on first-time visitors before midnight Monday, and (m) a redundant system for inviting church shoppers to place this new mission on their church shopping list.

A fifth response that overlaps the church shopper concept is those new missions that promise this will be an exciting new adventure. Part of their appeal is to those who have become "bored" with the style of worship and education in the church they have been in for years and have dropped out. Another part of the appeal is to venturesome and entrepreneurial laypersons who want to be challenged. Everything that is done in preparation for that first worship experience is designed to make this an exciting event. This includes the criteria used in selecting a temporary meeting place, the furnishings and lighting in that room, a high dependence on visual communication and humor, a fast-paced service, lively hymns, an excellent choir or orchestra (perhaps borrowed from a sponsoring church), relevant and dramatic preaching, and a carefully thought-through closing. The more exciting it is, the larger the proportion of first-time visitors who will return, the greater the pressure to "top that act" on the second Sunday, and the louder the criticism from those who believe the corporate worship of God should be slow-paced, dull, boring, and dreary.

In addition to a strong "anti-bored" stance, some of these new missions also promise a high degree of broad-based lay involvement in planning and leading corporate worship, in designing the total program, in formulating priorities, and in creating and implementing specialized forms of outreach.

IT'S 11 O'CLOCK ON SUNDAY MORNING, DO YOU KNOW WHERE YOUR CHURCH IS?

Sometimes a radically new approach is needed to reach the unchurched!
—FRIAR TUCK

A growing number of leaders engaged in planting new churches have concluded that no one approach is best. The best approach is a combination of several methodologies with a high degree of intentional redundancy.

Who will come, why will they come to help found a new worshiping community, and how will we reach them? Those are crucial questions, and the answers tend to create self-fulfilling prophecies.

CHAPTER EIGHT

Can Alexander Graham Bell Help Us?

One of the most divisive issues facing scores of congregations in the early years of the twentieth century was the telephone. Should we install a telephone in the church? What if it rings during worship? Who will answer it? Is it really an instrument of the Devil? A frequent compromise was to approve installation of a telephone in the church-owned house occupied by the minister, but to keep it out of the meeting house.

Once again in the final years of the twentieth century use of the telephone has become a divisive issue. It is now being hailed as a powerful aid in evangelism. Some will argue the biggest technological tool to impact new church development in the late 1970s and 1980s is telemarketing. In simple terms this replaces (or supplements) visitation evangelism with the telephone. The advantages are obvious. One person may complete four or five or perhaps a half dozen personal visits in two hours. By turning to the telephone that same individual can complete forty to seventy calls in two hours. It also eliminates the problem of access to guarded apartments and housing developments. Telemarketing can be an efficient means of eliminating from that list of prospective new members those persons actively involved in another church.

The first carefully designed experiment to use telemarketing in new church development was conducted in the late 1970s by the Reformed Church in America in the Dallas-Fort Worth area. Since then it has been utilized by hundreds of churches including new missions, congregations that are relocating their meeting place, and parishes that simply seek to expand their list of prospective members.

Telemarketing, as this procedure often is called, is a relatively simple, efficient, and attractive method for building a list of prospective future members. It works. It also has been oversold. Like every other approach, it does carry a price tag. The most obvious price tag is that it requires many telephone calls to produce one first-time visitor. Pastors utilizing telemarketing report they can expect one or two people will actually show up at worship for every one hundred to two hundred telephone calls completed. That is a highly respectable average, but that means ten to twenty thousand telephone calls (and in some communities that may be more like fifty thousand) to produce two hundred people for that first worship service.

Second, that is not simply ten thousand telephone calls. That is ten thousand *completed* telephone calls made by trained, skilled, friendly, articulate, persistent, patient, and persuasive callers.

Invasion of Privacy?

One group of pastors adamantly opposes use of the telephone as the primary tool for evangelism. They have had

An effective televangelism campaign recognizes it needs many calls to produce a single visitor!

—FRIAR TUCK

WHOA! DON'T HANG-UP! IT'LL TAKE TEN MORE CALLS to HEAR ANOTHER LIVE VOICE!

It is only the completed calls that produce prospects!

—FRIAR TUCK

their evening meal or a living room conversation with friends interrupted too often by the telephone call from a stranger wanting to sell them storm windows or magazine subscriptions. As a result of those unhappy experiences they refuse to inflict unsolicited telephone calls on strangers. They are convinced this is a gross invasion of privacy and is not in good taste. A growing number of people have made a personal commitment to refuse to purchase goods or services from telephone solicitors. (Ann Landers' column occasionally carries letters from these angry people.)

The other side of that argument is that it does work. If telephone solicitation did not "pay off," the people selling aluminum siding, gold coins, lawn care, stocks and bonds, magazine subscriptions, and storm windows would cease the practice. Likewise it can produce a long list of prospective new members with a modest investment of time and money. Do those benefits outweigh the invasion of privacy? Does the end justify the means? Is it acceptable to provoke the anger of a few in order to reach the many?

The Second Sunday Syndrome

Some will argue the invasion of privacy is an ideological issue and of minor concern. They raise the pragmatic question about what happens if it works. Perhaps the most common question that arises out of a successful telemarketing effort to produce a big crowd at that first worship service can be identified as the "Second Sunday Syndrome."

Thousands of friendly and persuasive telephone calls can produce a comparatively big crowd for that first Sunday morning. What happens the next Sunday? How can one be sure the second Sunday will have an equally large crowd? One answer, of course, is ten or twenty thousand telephone calls during those next five days. Another alternative is to invite a nationally famous minister to be the guest preacher on that second Sunday. A third alternative is to make a personal call on (a) every household represented at that first service and (b) every household where one or more members were absent from that first Sunday, but might be expected to be present on the second Sunday. A fourth alternative is to schedule that first Sunday for Palm Sunday on the assumption the natural appeal of Easter will produce a large crowd the following week.

A fifth alternative is to be prepared for a smaller crowd on succeeding Sundays and to respond creatively and positively to the negative psychological implications of shrinking attendance following that first Sunday of that new mission's life.

A sixth alternative is to identify, enlist, and train a cadre of volunteers to design and staff a full-scale Sunday morning program that will not only make most of those first-time visitors want to return the following Sunday but also attract addition-

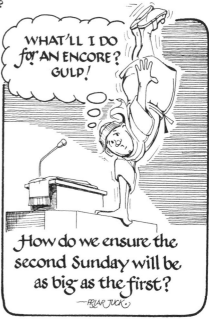

WHAT'LL I DO for AN ENCORE? GULP!

How do we ensure the second Sunday will be as big as the first?

—FRIAR TUCK

al first-time visitors. This should not only include a nursery for babies and a separate room for toddlers, but also a carefully rehearsed choir, an excellent sermon, meaningful prayers, a full-scale Sunday school for all ages, including adult classes with skilled and well-prepared teachers, plus a staffed fellowship period with refreshments both before and after worship.

A seventh, and overlapping, alternative is designed to respond to the fact that most of those first-time attenders who were invited by telephone will come expecting to be welcomed but may be greeted as strangers by most of those present. One effective means of overcoming this anonymity is to be sure every potential attender is called on personally by a staff member or a trained volunteer before that first Sunday so everyone will be greeted personally by someone who has met them earlier. A variation is to begin with week-night Bible study groups so most of those attending that first Sunday morning worship experience will already have been assimilated into a small caring group.

Perhaps the most effective alternative is to begin with an inspiring, relevant, and meaningful worship experience that not only makes all of those present want to return the following

LET'S BEGIN WITH REVELATION AND WORK FORWARD to GENESIS!

NEW MISSION BIBLE STUDY

Assimilation begins with that first Sunday (if not sooner)!

—FRIAR TUCK

Sunday, but also will compel many of them to invite unchurched friends, neighbors, and relatives to come with them on that second Sunday.

The Burden on the Pastor

This introduces what some mission developers contend is their biggest reservation about telemarketing. While these promises may never have been articulated by the callers, those being called may receive the impression they are being promised relevant, meaningful, and inspiring sermons, an exciting worship experience, outstanding music, and a caring and supportive fellowship of committed Christians prepared to welcome, love, and care for the lonely stranger. Some of those attracted by telemarketing apparently assume the pastor will be able and willing to spend an hour or two every week to become better acquainted with every prospective new member. At least a few new missions are not able to live up to those extravagant expectations, and after two or three visits, the sojourner never returns. Some of them find this experience reinforces their conviction that the churches promise more than they can deliver and that is an adequate reason to stay away.

For obvious reasons this disenchantment among first-time visitors is more likely to occur among those new missions started with one or two full-time church planters than in those that are launched with a team of three to seven full-time staff members.

How Much Rejection?

Scores of members who have volunteered to be part of a telemarketing effort raise another objection. This is rejection.

How much rejection can any one individual endure? The answer, of course, is, it varies. For some callers, this is an adventure, an opportunity to express their Christian witness and to win new converts. They enjoy using the telephone, and rejection rolls off them like water off a duck's back. For many others, however, this can become an onerous burden filled with rejection, scorn, and pain. While they may be fully committed Christians, that commitment does not automatically make them persuasive sales agents to people who are hostile in responding to this

unsolicited invasion of their privacy. Since the words of rejection may be heard far more frequently than the words of interest, gratitude, or acceptance, this can be a distressing experience for the caller. One alternative is a careful screening of the volunteers for calling. Another is to provide the support system to help the volunteers cope with this rejection. A third is for those seasoned, persuasive, tough, and highly committed volunteers to make that first round of calls and for other callers to make the second round. This, of course, undercuts any feeling of continuity the initial caller may have created.

Who Responds?

Who responds to the telemarketing approach to new church development? The reflections of pastors and church planters who have used this system suggest that most of the respondents fall into one of eight overlapping categories.

1. The dropouts and inactives who have been contemplating "coming back to church," but needed the impetus of that friendly and persuasive telephone call to move them out of their passive

state. This category includes young newlyweds, parents whose first-born child is now ready for Sunday school, young single adults, and people beginning a second marriage.

2. Lonely people who seek acceptance and comfort and want to be loved.

3. Newcomers to the community who are still church shopping.

4. Venturesome, outgoing, and risk-taking adults who enjoy helping pioneer the new, but display little interest when asked to maintain old institutions.

5. Adults with psychological problems who are seeking one-to-one counseling.

6. People who have felt they were rejected from other churches because of life-style, race, physical disabilities, or their belief system, including those who have been unable to find a church that agrees with their system of biblical interpretation.

7. Churchgoers who are dissatisfied with (a) their own congregation and/or (b) their current pastor and/or (c) the public stance of their denomination.

8. People on a religious pilgrimage who are attracted by the possibility that this new mission will become a destination for them, not simply a brief stop on an endless journey.

The larger the proportion of respondents who come from categories 2, 5, 6, 7, and 8, the heavier and the more complex the work load for that church planter. This is another argument for beginning with a staff of three to seven full-time people if telemarketing is to be the primary tool for reaching prospective future members. That also may be an explanation for some of the positive reports from relocating congregations on telemarketing.

Should We Use It?

While the decision to use the telephone as the primary tool for building a list of prospective new members obviously rests with those who will make the policy decisions about launching that new mission, it merits careful consideration for use in the following situations:

1. When the mission-developer pastor is not convinced that invasion of privacy is a barrier to its use.

2. When this is seen as only one of several means of building a list of prospective new members.

3. When those responsible are prepared to carefully plan the follow-up stages that normally include attractive direct mailings to everyone on that list of prospective new members and personal visits that will offset the sense of anonymity inherent in televangelism.

4. When the mission-developer pastor is an extroverted personality who also is an exceptionally productive worker, enjoys meeting strangers, displays a high level of skill in correctly remembering the names of strangers, is an excellent preacher, is able to design and lead exciting worship experiences, and excels in creating and nurturing the group life of a new congregation.

NOT ANGRY ANSWERS, LONG HOURS OR THE SLAMMING *of* RECEIVERS WILL KEEP US FROM SPREADING THE LOVE OF GOD!

Televangelism is not for the cold-hearted, cynical, or cowardly!

—FRIAR TUCK.

or

5. When the team of church planters includes at least three full-time people who together possess the skills and gifts described above.

These considerations also should be factors in the decision to use telemarketing in (a) congregations relocating to construct a new meeting house as part of a larger effort to launch a new era in ministry and (b) long-established congregations launching new ministries to reach the unchurched.

Telemarketing is a comparatively new tool and, like most new tools, it has both advantages and disadvantages.

CHAPTER NINE

Should We Use Direct Mail?

"Here's our fifty dollars, and if you want to see a cheerful giver, look at me," declared Pat Callahan. "Give me a choice between writing a check for fifty dollars and making five hundred telephone calls, I'll give you the money every time!"

"What's the matter? Didn't you enjoy your part of our telephone crusade?" questioned Jack Gallego as he accepted the check. "The forty of us who volunteered for the crusade made nearly 20,000 telephone calls, and we did identify close to a hundred prospective future members. You should feel proud of yourself for your contribution to that effort, Pat. I thought it was a success, and I enjoyed witnessing to Christ as I talked with my five hundred."

"Maybe you enjoyed it, but I didn't," replied Pat. "I never dreamed there were so many rude people out there. Some of them swore at me, two or three blew a whistle so loudly into their telephone it almost pierced my eardrums, at least a hundred hung up on me before I could finish my opening sentence, and a bunch of others reprimanded me for the invasion of their privacy. Several others replied by bragging about their church and told me that instead of starting one more unneeded church, in what already is an overchurched community, I should come to their church. The only other time in my life I ever felt such rejection was when I used to be the last one picked when we chose up sides to play softball back in elementary school."

"Well, that's all behind us now. I think you'll enjoy this new campaign," declared Jack. "As you know, we've decided to use direct mail as our second effort to enlist new members, and we've asked each family to contribute fifty dollars to cover the printing and postage. Next month we're going to send an invitational brochure to every household in these two zip code areas. Your fifty dollars will cover the cost of printing and mailing about four hundred brochures. If you have any ideas for a second mailing we'll be doing later in the fall, let me know."

* * *

"I'll bring you the brochure we got in the mail the other day. I think I still have it," offered Robin Byrd to the newest member of that five-person car pool. "Right after we moved here, we joined First Presbyterian Church, and we're happy there, so we're not in the market for a new church home. When this brochure came in the mail the other day, I was so impressed with it, I laid it aside to show my dad who's coming to see us in a couple of weeks. He chairs the evangelism committee in the church I grew up in, and I thought he would be interested in it. The brochure describes a new church that just started a couple of months ago, and it invites you to come to their first Christmas Eve service next month. It sounds like an attractive church, and it may be just what you're looking for. I'll be sure to bring it along tomorrow."

* * *

"Would you please tell me the name of your company again?" asked Harold Hassey in a quiet voice as he reached for a pencil with his right hand while holding the telephone in his left hand. "Thank you for repeating that," he said as he finished writing. "My wife and I agreed a long time ago that we would never patronize any firm that interrupted our dinner with unsolicited telephone calls, and I wanted to be sure I had the correct name of your company."

* * *

These three conversations illustrate three reasons why some new missions prefer direct mail over telemarketing. Direct mail eliminates the invasion of privacy issue. The recipient can examine that piece of direct mail at his or her convenience or discard it without even opening. It is far more difficult to ignore the ring of the telephone, even during a meal or while cleaning out the basement. Direct mail can be examined on the recipient's schedule and at the recipient's discretion. Rarely does direct mail arouse hostile responses. The senders of direct mail do not have to respond to rejection, profanity, hostility, insults, and rudeness.

The interested recipient of direct mail has a tangible item that can be passed on to someone else. That piece of paper can be referred to later. It is not as vulnerable to misunderstanding or to being misquoted as a telephone message.

A Fundamental Difference

For many sincere Christians the fundamental distinction between direct mail and use of the telephone is of basic importance. Do I, as a Christian, begin with my agenda, and at my convenience approach someone else with my witness to Jesus Christ as Lord and Savior? Or do I try to be more sensitive to the recipient's concerns, schedule, and availability? Proponents of direct mail tend to choose the second of these two alternatives. One model of this second approach can be found repeatedly in the first four books of the New Testament as Jesus repeatedly approached individuals on their agenda, asking, "Where do you hurt?"

The Cost Benefit Question

If a new mission can find and utilize a bank of telephones at no charge and if that new mission can enlist and train a cadre of twenty to fifty volunteers to make several hundred telephone calls each, that clearly is less expensive that direct mail.

If, however, the new mission must pay for the use of that set of telephones and/or if the time and energy of the volunteer callers is given an economic value, the costs of bulk rate direct mail and telephone evangelism are comparable. Direct mail does require an initial capital investment for the cost of that bulk rate mailing permit, and the accumulation of that initial mailing list (unless the mail is sent to every box-holder).

The long-term response rates usually are about the same, perhaps slightly higher for direct mail. One of the benefits of direct mail, however, is the cumulative impact as the mailing list is built, refined, classified, purged, and revised. Once that system has been developed, a second mailing requires a modest investment of the time of volunteers compared to a second round of telephone calls.

Should We Use Direct Mail?

When and to Whom?

When does a new mission use direct mail? What kind of invitations do people receive via direct mail?[1] Human ingenuity and creativity mean the answer is a list without end, but a few examples illustrate the possibilities.

YES, VIRGINIA, WE OFFER MORE FLAVORS THAN VANILLA!

WORSHIP and STUDY OPPORTUNIT

SUNDAY MORNINGS:
WORSHIP: 7-8:30-10-NOON
STUDY: 7-8:30-10-NOON
WEEKDAYS:
7 AM and 7 P.M.
SATURDAYS:
ALL-DAY RETREATS
FIND SOME FRIENDS AND WE'LL PROVIDE A TEACHER!

Growing churches offer people choices!
—FRIAR TUCK.

1. An invitation to serve on the planning committee to help plant a new church.

2. An invitation to help pioneer a new Tuesday evening Bible study group that will be one of the foundations for this new mission.

3. An invitation to serve on the planning committee to help design that first worship experience.

4. An invitation to help plan the Sunday school for that new mission.

5. An invitation to help pioneer a new choir or an orchestra for this new church.

6. An invitation to help plan the Christmas Eve program for that first Christmas Eve service (or services).

7. An invitation to come, to worship with us, and to help pioneer the starting of a new congregation in this community.

8. An invitation to come and help design an after-school ministry with children for one day a week during the school year.

9. An invitation to those who are seeking a place to worship on Christmas Eve to come worship with us. (This is planned for what is the biggest reentry point into the church for adults who dropped out of church years ago.)

10. An invitation to enroll your child in the newest Sunday school in town—our first Sunday is next Sunday, and your child can help pioneer this new adventure.

11. An invitation to those who are home all day with a brand

101

I THINK I'M GETTING THE POINT!

Direct mail is the most effective and efficient means of reaching the unchurched!

—FRIAR TUCK—

CHRISTMAS ALWAYS ATTRACTS THE WISE!

Christmas Eve serves many of the unchurched as a portal of re-entry!

—FRIAR TUCK—

new baby for the first time in their life, to come and help pioneer the creation of a new Mother's Club that will meet for the first time next Tuesday at ten o'clock in the morning at suchandsuch a place. If you need a ride or simply want more information, call this number.

12. An invitation to newlyweds and/or to those who are part of an interdenominational or interfaith marriage to share in the creation of a new church that is bringing together people from a variety of religious backgrounds.

13. An invitation to be a member of a mission work team this congregation is assembling to go on a ten-day mission work camp experience.

14. An invitation to help create the kind of adult Sunday school class you've been seeking but never found.

15. An invitation to help create a new church for that new generation of churchgoers born after 1955. If you were born in 1955 or earlier, please ignore this invitation.

Every new mission has several distinctive assets that can be identified by such terms as "new," "help pioneer," "openness," "participation," "a chance to create the new," and "easy entry." These assets should not be ignored.

Redundancy and Mailing Lists

Two of the central themes in the use of direct mail are redundancy and mailing lists. Everyone who has been identified as a potential future member should receive at least one mailing every month. One purpose of that first huge bulk mailing is to build a smaller list of potential future members. Every possible source should be utilized to expand that list of potential future members.

MY JUNK MAIL WANTS ME *to* BUY! THE CHURCH INVITES ME *to* COME!

THEIR MAIL

Mailing monthly to prospects is less offensive and more productive than unsolicited phone calls!
—FRIAR TUCK

This includes those who appear in response to a mailing or who telephone for more information. It includes every person in every class, committee, choir, and special program as well as every attender at worship. It includes the names and addresses of persons identified as potential future members by that early cadre of volunteers. It includes the names of those who offered a positive response when called on personally.

As time goes by, that mailing list should be divided so special mailings can be sent to teenagers or to one-time visitors or to recent newcomers to that community or to new parents or to new empty-nest couples. Most special mailings should be made to every resident who fits that category. Thus that invitation to help pioneer a new Mother's Club should be sent to every woman who gave birth to a baby in the past year. That invitation to help pioneer a new first-grade Sunday school class should go to every first-grader in every school (both private and public) in that community as well as to every home schooler in first grade. That invitation to help pioneer a new high school youth choir should go to every high school youth in that community. Incidentally, one of the advantages of direct mail is that those letters can be

103

mailed to *every* box-holder or household. By contrast, in 1989, 29 percent of all American households had an unlisted telephone number, up from 22 percent in 1984. That figure also is approximately the same as those who report a hostile response to "junk telephone calls" or who identify as one of their "pet peeves" receiving a sales call during dinner or telephone solicitations using prerecorded messages.[2]

In each case those who respond go on the mailing list for future mailings to that slice of the population.

Redundancy and specialized mailing lists are two of the keys in making direct mail a useful tool in church planting.

CHAPTER TEN

Twelve Questions on Identity

"When I moved to central Texas from northern New Jersey fourteen years ago to start this new mission, I quickly discovered that I needed to identify with this part of the world," reflected John Buchanon, the founding pastor of a congregation now averaging well over four hundred at Sunday morning worship. "Most of the churches in my denomination are in the North and the West, and I felt something like a pioneer out on the frontier. I also found a lot of other displaced people here in central Texas, people who moved here because of job opportunities. I concluded that if I wanted to start a new church, I should identify with the other adults who also were new to this community. It didn't take long for me to learn that many of these newcomers placed their initial allegiance in the public school system in general and the high school football team in particular. The primary personal allegiance was not to their job, that was a business or professional allegiance, not personal. It also was not to this city. This municipality was incorporated in 1927 and for decades was a small rural community. About eighteen years ago the population began to increase very rapidly and today the total is five times what it was in 1970, but control is largely in the hands of the old-timers or of native Texans. It still is hard to get elected to public office if you come from the North. Therefore, the recent newcomers rarely identify with the city. They identify with the public school system first of all, the church second, their job third, and this city maybe tenth."

"What did that mean to you as you started a new church here?" inquired a visitor from Indiana. "I also notice you did not mention denominational loyalties."

"That's right," agreed John. "Maybe 10 percent of our first two hundred members came from my denomination. For the Southern Baptists, the Churches of Christ, the Presbyterians, the

105

Disciples of Christ, the Episcopalians, the Methodists, and maybe the Lutherans that denominational allegiance could be important here, but not for us. We have been successful in reaching newcomers without much regard to denominational background. Very few of our members rank denominational identity high on that list of their institutional loyalties.

"My response to that fact of life," continued John Buchanon, "was to attempt to meet people on their agenda, not mine. I arrived in late July, and I doubt if I have missed six home football games in fourteen years. I joined the Parent-Teacher Organization and twice I've served as president. That's where I first met a lot of the people who subsequently joined this church. This is a big school district and includes thirty-one school principals. Six of them are members of this congregation. Four years ago I was elected to the local school board, and now I'm vice-president of the board. Beginning with my second year in Texas we always designate the first Sunday in September every year to honor the educators for their labor in this community. That Sunday usually is our fourth highest attendance of the year. Easter, Christmas Eve, and Palm Sunday are the only times we have a bigger crowd. Personally I am a strong proponent of the public school system, so I have no philosophical or ideological problems with this approach. If I were asked to start a new church in your state, I would do the same thing."

"You might substitute basketball for football if you were in Indiana," suggested the visitor. "What other distinguishing factors would you lift up from your fourteen years here?"

"Three others immediately come to mind," replied John. "The first was a mistake I made. As I told you, I arrived in July and immediately scheduled our first worship service for five weeks later. That was too soon. We had well over a hundred people on our first Sunday, but that dropped to fifty-eight on our second Sunday. We attracted a lot of people who wanted to be part of a small church, and many of them subsequently resisted our efforts to grow. Some of them eventually left as we grew. If I had to do it over again, I would try to begin with at least two hundred and avoid the risk of attracting those who are looking for a small church.

"Second," continued John, "is the age stratification that often comes with being a new church in a new residential community.

That's a natural phenomenon, I guess, but I resented it. For the first decade nearly all our adult members were between twenty-seven and fifty years old. Lately we've become more of an intergenerational church, but that bothered me for a long time.

"Third, one of the things that attracted me to this assignment was that I knew two of the other ministers who also were starting new churches. One is a Presbyterian minister who was my neighbor in my first pastorate and we had become good friends. The second was a seminary classmate who came here to start a new church two years before I arrived. While we come from different denominations, we were friends in seminary. I came with the dream of collegial relationships with these two neighboring pastors. We worked at that pretty hard for the first several months I was here. Each one of them was experiencing some problems and a sense of loneliness. We met together nearly every Tuesday morning for Bible study, prayer, and sermon preparation for the first several months after I arrived. It wasn't too long, however, before two of us realized that really wasn't working. We had too many other claims on our loyalties, our time, and our energy. In effect, I swapped that relationship for a more active role in the P.T.O. One of the other two also was ready to drop out because his congregation had reached the point of constructing their first unit. He found that took an awful lot of time and we could see that also was his new lover. We were the first wife who was being abandoned in favor of that sexy young chick the husband meets at the office. So one day we agreed by mutual consent to shift from meeting every Tuesday morning to once a quarter. We don't quite do that, but two of us do get together twice a year. The other guy moved about seven years ago."

These comments from a veteran mission-developer pastor illustrate seven of a dozen questions that are a part of planting a new church. All twelve can be grouped under the word "identity." In one way or another all twelve reflect the search for a distinctive identity for that new mission. Perhaps the simplest example of that natural and predictable search for identity is the need for a name. This is one of the first questions asked the mother after the birth of that baby. This is one of the most urgent questions raised when a child is given a pet. This is the question asked of the high school senior going on to school, "What's the name of the school you plan to attend?" Today this identity question often is asked of brides. "Will you take your husband's name or keep your own or hyphenate the two names or will you both take a new name?" This also soon becomes a pressing question for the founders of the new church. For many of us a central part of our identity is in our name.

Who Is the Minister?

The previous chapters underscore the central role of the church planter or mission-developer pastor in organizing a new congregation. The choice of that person usually is the most critical decision in launching a new mission! Frequently, the identity of that new church is a reflection of the personality, gifts, gender, values, experience, nationality, race, education, priorities, family status, political views, theological stance, social class, age, and hobbies of the pastor.

If the personality and culture of that new mission reflect the pastor, this raises a question about the minister's identity. How does that church planter gain a sense of identity with that community? What is the community image of that mission developer? How do other people see this stranger who has come in to create a new congregation? Where does this pastor meet and make new friends?

In yesterday's world a common answer to that question was for the associate minister on the staff of First Church to lead a nucleus consisting of several families out to found a new congregation on the edge of the city. The identity of those pioneers was in the group, in the support from that sponsoring congregation, in the denominational affiliation, in this adventure, and in their leaders.

A different and often highly productive response is illustrated by the comments of John Buchanon, who saw himself as a displaced person and shared with other displaced persons by meeting and making new friends through participation in the affairs of the public school system.

This identification as a community leader can be an especially useful role for pastors in two radically different settings. One is the senior minister of the downtown church. The other is the church planter.

A third response is the mission developer who identifies with that initial cadre of pioneers. That group may become the pastor's surrogate family as well as primary point of identification with people in that community. This can be highly effective if the goal is to build a relatively small *Gemeinschaft*-type congregation.

A much rarer alternative is for the church planter to use the local media to create an identity in that place. This may include a weekly essay in the local newspaper, frequent appearances on the local radio station, interviews or programs on the public access channel of the cable television system, membership in a service club, speeches to local community organizations, and active participation in the local ministerial association.

For at least a few church planters the response to this issue of creating a local identity in what usually is a new setting is to avoid it by allocating discretionary time to activities that involve out-of-town trips. This may include an active role in denominational meetings or travel or hobbies or visits with geographically scattered family members or frequent trips "back home."

How a church planter goes about identifying with that new community can be an influential factor in determining who joins that new mission.

Collegial, Team, or Unilateral?

Moving to a strange community with the assignment to launch a new congregation can be an extremely lonely task. This can be an especially lonely assignment for the unmarried minister who returns to an empty house every night. One of the disconcerting facets of this lonely experience can be the discovery that no one in that community asked you to come and organize a new church. It also can be a lonely role for the wife of the male church planter.

109

... it can be a
lonely experience
for a
church planter's family!
—FRIAR TUCK

When she and her husband left that supportive, loving, and caring congregation for this new adventure, she also left behind a support group that may not be replaced for years.

One ancient response to this loneliness factor was to ask the associate minister of First Church to organize that new church and to enlist a group of supportive members to constitute that initial cadre.

A more recent approach, which has an ancient historical base, is to expect the mission developer to identify with a group of ministers. One model of this arrangement met together weekly in the chapter room of the English cathedral in the twelfth century. A more recent model was the group ministry in which several members of the clergy created a mutual support group to minister together in the inner city or in rural America. Usually the accountability of the individual ministers was to that group. The group recruited and admitted new members and also acted on issues related to the departure of a member. Typically these groups followed the centuries-old model of weekly gatherings for prayer, Bible study, accountability, and policy making. This collegial approach to ministry means that a big chunk of a pastor's identity is in that group.

Experience suggests (a) it is difficult to sustain these groups without active denominational support, (b) these groups tend to erode rapidly following the departure of the last original member, (c) they work best when all the ministers see themselves as sojourners in a strange land and thus find it easier to identify with the group than with the members of the individual congregation, and (d) the entrepreneurial personality, who often is the most effective church planter, tends to display limited long-term interest in this collegial model. These ministers usually are more comfortable identifying with the community and their congregation than with a group of clergypersons. John Buchanon represents that pattern.

A third approach, which displays many of the marks of the collegial concept, is to send a team of three-to-seven full-time and/or part-time persons in to organize what from day one is designed to be a large congregation. In effect, the goal is to create a large multiple-staff church that will be self-governing, self-supporting, and self-propagating by month twelve. This can be the lowest cost

LET'S SEE, I BRUSHED MY TEETH, PUT-ON DEODORANT...

ALL PASTORS' BIBLE STUDY

A successful pastor today may not be appreciated by his or her peers!
—FRIAR TUCK

approach to new church development, it is a positive response to the question of where does that new church developer find a sense of identity, and it reduces the problem of loneliness.

The fourth, and perhaps the most widely hoped for response to this question, is to enlist the psychologically healthy, inner-directed, future-oriented, goal-driven, self-confident, experienced, entrepreneurial, competent, happy, extroverted, enterprising, gregarious, skilled, highly committed, and wise pastor to be the mission developer and pursue a unilateral approach.

Which of these four alternatives is a part of your strategy for organizing new churches?

The Displaced People Syndrome

John Buchanon saw himself as a displaced person when he left New Jersey to go to Texas to organize a new church. He identified with the other displaced people and met many of them on what they identified as comfortable turf. This was an effective strategy.

This also raises one of the critical, but frequently overlooked questions in identifying the potential constituency for a new congregation. Frequently, it is obscured by the naive declaration, "Our goal is to reach and serve all the unchurched people out here." While that statement has a noble ring to it, in fact it ranks somewhere between presumptuous and stupid if the goal is to formulate an effective strategy for church planting.

The most obvious fallacy in that declaration is that no one church can reach and serve all the "unchurched."

A second limitation of that declaration is that a large proportion of people who identify themselves as committed believers in Jesus Christ as Lord and Savior are insulted when they are identified by some pious stranger as "unchurched." The fact that they currently are not involved in the life of any worshiping community does not make them "unchurched." At least thirty million Americans, age eighteen and over, who are not carried on the membership rosters of any worshiping community, identify themselves as members of a particular religious body.

A third and far more critical problem with that declaration is, Which unchurched people are you seeking to reach? Those who have never made a profession of faith? Residents who are the adult children of parents born in Mexico? Dropouts? Immigrants from Latin America? Church members who have been excommunicated? The bored? The pilgrims on a religious journey? The disillusioned? Newcomers to that community? Immigrants from the Pacific Rim?

A useful conceptual framework is the one identified by John Buchanon. One of the most effective routes to travel in planting a new church is to seek to identify with, reach, and serve the newcomers who see themselves as displaced people. This was the central organizing principle in founding tens of thousands of German Lutheran, Swedish Baptist, Welsh Presbyterian, Dutch Reformed, Armenian Congregational, Norwegian Lutheran, German Baptist, Italian Methodist, Swedish Lutheran, Scotch Presbyterian, Volga German Congregational, German Methodist, Irish Catholic, Japanese Methodist, Danish Lutheran, Swedish Methodist, Romanian Baptist, Hawaiian Congregational, and Italian Catholic congregations between 1700 and 1920.

The contemporary parallel can be found in the success stories of new churches founded to reach displaced Puerto Ricans in New Jersey, displaced northern Lutherans in Arizona, displaced Roman Catholics on Staten Island, displaced Koreans in Chicago, displaced northern Presbyterians in South Carolina, displaced Cubans in Florida, displaced Japanese in California, and displaced urban Episcopalians in suburbia. It has been far more difficult to build a new congregation from adults who came to Texas to make some money and plan to return to Mexico to spend it. It is much easier to create that new worshiping community with displaced people who expect to remain in this place.

For thousands of new missions the dominant identity is a reflection of two overlapping themes. The first is that these

TONIGHT'S MEETING WILL BEGIN WITH A TREASURE HUNT...

WE'RE LOOKING FOR THE...
✶ HOMELESS
✶ HELPLESS
✶ HUNGRY
✶ HOPELESS
✶ HELL-BENT, ETC.

Our agenda will be found in the needs of those outside the church!

— FRIAR TUCK ©

are self-identified displaced people. Second, they share a common identity in terms of place of birth, race, language, social class, national heritage, previous place of residence, value system, or theological perspective that causes them to believe they would not be welcomed in the existing churches in that community and/or those churches could not be responsive to their religious needs.

By contrast, it is far, far, far more difficult to reach, attract, and enlist as new members in a new mission adults who have been living in the same dwelling for a decade or longer and who are not involved in the ongoing life of any religious body. (One of the keys to reaching this slice of the adult population is to create an exceptionally attractive and exciting Sunday school.)

A third facet of this scenario is one followed by many church planters. This is to reach, attract, and enlist as future members a different group of displaced people. These are the individuals who are members of a church in that community but who either have dropped out or are about to drop out of that congregation. They may have been hurt, disillusioned, insulted, neglected, or overworked and underappreciated. In other cases, they continued as active members until the youngest child was confirmed or

113

left home. A fair number drop out because they are disenchanted with the new minister. (This is one of the arguments for long pastorates.) A growing number see themselves on a religious pilgrimage and recently they realized their journey was taking them in one direction while their church was heading down a different road. For others divorce and/or remarriage is the primary reason for leaving.

Many of these displaced people are longtime residents in that community but feel they need to find a new church home. At least a few are challenged by the dream of helping pioneer something new before they become too old to make a significant contribution by their presence, their prayers, their work, and their gifts.

If the goal is to reach longtime residents who are seeking a new church home, it makes sense to begin with a nucleus of discontented members who are eager to leave the sponsoring church to go out and help found a new congregation that will be closer to what they are seeking. If, however, the goal is to reach newcomers to the community who feel repelled by the long-established churches, it may not be wise to attempt to clone the mother church with a carbon copy daughter built around a cadre of longtime residents.

Which of these groups of displaced persons in the local population do you identify as the largest source of your future members for this new mission?

The Denominational Identity

Back in the 1880s approximately two-thirds of all new churches were affiliated with what today are six religious bodies (United Methodist, National Baptist Convention, Southern Baptist Convention, Roman Catholic Church, Evangelical Lutheran Church in America, and the Presbyterian Church [U.S.A.]). During the 1980s these six religious bodies accounted for approximately one-fifth of all new congregations—and the Southern Baptists were responsible for nearly one-half of that one-fifth.

Today a growing proportion of new churches do not carry a denominational identification. Many are independent or nondenominational congregations. Others are affiliated with a denomination, but see that as a handicap in reaching displaced people and minimize the visibility of that denominational identity. This is in sharp contrast to the 1950s when most new churches flaunted their denominational label.

As you plan your strategy for organizing a new church, will you emphasize or minimize that denominational identity? If you do not lift up a denominational affiliation, what will be the central themes in communicating your identity to outsiders?

Gemeinschaft or Gesellschaft?

As John Buchanon reflected on his fourteen years in that new church in Texas, he regretted the decision to begin with a relatively small number of people that first summer. A useful conceptual framework for examining this facet of identity was described by a German sociologist, Ferdinand Tönnies, a century ago in his famous book *Gemeinschaft und Gesellschaft.* In this landmark study the author identified the small community that is built largely on one-to-one relationships with the family as a cornerstone as *Gemeinschaft.* Typically these small communities display a notable degree of homogeneity and place a high value on interpersonal relationships, place, a common language, kinship ties, bloodlines, friendships, morality, land, traditions, virtue, respect, customs, loyalty, mutual support, and coopera- tion. The typical small town in rural America in 1923 was a living example of *Gemeinschaft* and most Protestant churches reflected that expression of human relationships.

During the past four decades a large proportion of new churches have been started around this definition of community. Unlike John Buchanon's experience, this approach to new church development often results in a congregation that eventually plateaus in size with fewer than one hundred sixty people at worship.

By contrast, an increasing number of church planters have utilized a different conceptual model of human relationships. Their efforts parallel what Tönnies identified as *Gesellschaft.* In this description of the world the basic building blocks are not individuals and families, but rather associations, groups, cor- porations, institutions, business, legal obligations, rationality, intentionality, and offices or titles.

Many of today's large Protestant congregations reflect that

115

form of relationships. Rarely can any one person call every other member correctly by name, and these parishes really are a federation of classes, boards, organizations, groups, choirs, departments, cells, commissions, committees, task forces, programs, and ministries.

An English synonym for *Gemeinschaft* is community. For *Gesellschaft* the English synonym is society. The one-room country school of 1935 was an example of *Gemeinschaft*. The huge consolidated high school of 1991 symbolizes *Gesellschaft*.

Sooner or later every new church takes on the characteristics of an institution. As you build this new congregation, do you identify with *Gemeinschaft* as the ideal model of human relationships? Or do you identify the future with *Gesellschaft*? The latter model typically means that eventually this will become a congregation of subgroups that often exist in considerable tension with one another and that occasionally erupts into open conflict.

The conflict over identity often surfaces when someone suggests the time has come to schedule two worship services for Sunday morning. Those who identify with the *Gemeinschaft* view of human relationships will urge that we build a sanctuary that will be sufficiently large to accommodate the entire congregation at one service. The *Gesellschaft* crowd may ask, "You are planning for these to be two *different* worship experiences, aren't you?" or "Perhaps we should be planning for three services, not two?"

Today's megachurches that represent a *Gesellschaft* perspective on the world often arouse negative reactions among those who see *Gemeinschaft* as the ideal synonym for "worshiping community."

Back in the early years of the twentieth century, when the average (mean) size of Protestant congregations in the United States ranged between sixty and one hundred fifty members, the *Gemeinschaft* definition of community was consistent with reality.*

---

*In 1906 the (mean) average size of the 1,755 congregations in the Evangelical Association was 64 members; in the Southern Baptist the average was 95 members per congregation; for the Congregationalists it was 123; for Northern Baptists 128; Disciples of Christ 120; Methodist Episcopal Church 100; Methodist Protestant Church 63; Methodist Episcopal Church, South 93; Colored Methodist Episcopal Church 73; Presbyterian Church in the United States of America 148; Presbyterian Church in the United States 86; National Baptist Convention 95; African Methodist Episcopal Church 85; Protestant Episcopal Church 132; and all Lutheran parishes 166.

In today's world, when the generations of Americans born after 1945 are showing up in disproportionately large numbers in congregations averaging more than eight hundred at worship, the *Gesellschaft* view of human relationships may be more attractive to those formulating a strategy for new church development.

Which Generation?

While it rarely receives the attention it merits, one of the most influential facets of the identity of a new mission is reflected in the age of the first hundred members. Frequently, the vast majority of adult charter members are drawn from two generations. A new mission in a retirement community in Florida or New Jersey might be designed to reach the generations born before 1930 while a new suburban church in Illinois might focus on the generations born after 1955.

The most obvious implication of this facet of identity is in the choice of a temporary meeting place. The new mission designed to reach younger parents with elementary age children may choose to meet for a year or two in a public elementary school building. The new mission designed to reach adults born in the first third of the twentieth century may choose the club house at the golf course for a temporary meeting place. The church planter seeking to reach the "sight-sound-sensation" generations born after 1955 may choose a motion picture theater as the temporary meeting place.

A second implication is in the selection of a mission-developer pastor. Although many exceptions exist, pastors born in the 1928–42 era often have been most effective in building an intergenerational congregation. Those born in the 1942–55 era may be less effective in reaching adults born in the first third of the twentieth century.

Another implication is in the financing of the capital improvements. The new mission designed to reach and serve people born in the first four decades of the twentieth century is more likely to concentrate on contributions from accumulated wealth in the capital funds appeal while the congregation designed to serve people born after 1955 is more likely to seek pledges from current income.

117

SURELY, HOPEFULLY, SOMEONE OUT THERE LIKES ME!

SLAM!

Often, a divided church can result in the multiplication of new saints!

— FRIAR TUCK

How will generational differences shape the identity of your new congregation and influence policy decisions?

Believers or Non-believers?

Overlapping the issue raised earlier about displaced people is another central question about identity. From 1860 through the 1960s, a large proportion of new churches in North America were established to reach "our people who are moving into this community." This pattern included the thousands of churches designed to reach and serve the immigrants from Europe as well as the people moving from the central city to the suburbs. After World War II that pattern was extended to serve northern churchgoers moving to the South and West. In other words, believers founded new churches to reach and serve other believers. The most obvious manifestation of that pattern was the religious census taken to test whether sufficient numbers of believers of "our" religious persuasion lived here to justify the investment in starting a new mission.

The past three or four decades have brought a sharp increase in the number of new congregations created to reach non-believers. This approach requires a radically different approach and in several dozen places has produced a new congregation that soon passed the five-hundred mark in average worship attendance. One reason behind that rapid growth was that the non-believer grapevine carried the challenge to come and see what is happening here. Those non-believers who did come had access to and credibility in that non-believer grapevine.

It is not uncommon for church planters to declare their goal is to reach non-believers, but by their actions they may seek out committed Christians who are newcomers to that community in order to have the assistance of a cadre of informed, committed, experienced, skilled, and supportive volunteer workers.

In addition, and far more significant, the mission designed to reach the non-believer and the new Christian usually offers a different type of worship experience than the church designed to reach believers. By definition most long-established congregations communicate the image they welcome believers.

Finally, the church planter organizing a new congregation designed to reach believers will be subject to far greater pressures to schedule that first worship service as early as possible than will be felt by the mission developer who is seeking to build a new church from people who are non-believers, inquirers, curious skeptics, and completely inactive former churchgoers. That Tuesday evening Bible study group may satisfy the wants of this group of pioneers for many months.

As you plan your strategy for planting a new church, will you seek to identify with those churches designed for believers? Or will you project an identity suggesting this is a place that welcomes non-believers? The first test of that will be in whether your first hundred worshipers are largely longtime believers and perhaps even second- or third-generation Christians. Or will most of that first hundred people be a mixture of self-identified non-believers, dropouts, searchers, seekers, people on a religious quest, new Christians, and inquirers?

How will the general community identify this new mission? As a place for those who are committed Christians to help pioneer a new church? Or as a venture designed to bring the Good News of Jesus Christ to non-believers?

The first approach is compatible with the idea of beginning with a core of veteran Christians sent out by a sponsoring church. That may not be a wise beginning point, however, if the primary audience for this new church is the non-believing slice of the population.

High Demand or Voluntary Association?

One of the crucial questions on identity that should be decided early concerns expectations. Will this congregation project high expectations of every person seeking to become a member? Or

MEET OUR NEW CHAIRPERSON OF EVANGELISM!

Our approach needs to be quite different when addressing non-believers!

—FRIAR TUCK

will it resemble a voluntary association in which members determine for themselves their degree of involvement, their support, and their allegiance?

A simple illustration is the new mission that requires not only a profession of faith or believer's baptism as the initiating rite, but also requires all members to participate in corporate worship two or three times every week, to return to the Lord a tithe of their income through that church, to share in a weekly Bible study group, and to contribute time and talents as a volunteer. In these high demand churches it is not uncommon for the worship attendance to be triple or quadruple the reported member figure.

By contrast, other churches project modest expectations beyond that initial profession of faith, and the membership figure greatly exceeds the average attendance at Sunday morning worship.

Will prospective members identify your new mission as a high expectation church or one that resembles a voluntary organization?

Commuter or Community?

"We recruited sixty volunteers to canvass this neighborhood door-to-door and they found seventy-three families who stated they might be interested in joining a new Presbyterian church if one were started here," explained a man who had taken the initiative in pressing for a new Presbyterian church in the neighborhood in which he resided.

* * *

"We purchased a twenty-three-acre parcel of land at an interchange on the north-south expressway that carries a large number of people from their homes to work every day," explained a denominational official responsible for new church development. "It is a highly visible site and easily accessible with good topography. We expect this will become a three-thousand-member church before the turn of the century."

WE'VE GOT AMPLE SPACE, BUT THE BENEDICTION MUST COME BEFORE the POPCORN'S BUTTERED!

MATINEE - 1 P.M.

TICKETS

ALL AGES CHURCH SCHOOL 9:30 AM WORSHIP 11 O'CLOCK

—FRIAR TUCK—

Where we temporarily meet has permanent implications!

The first approach is compatible with the dream of organizing a relatively small *Gemeinschaft* congregation that will serve one slice of the residents of that residential neighborhood. The second is compatible with the dream of creating a large multiple-staff *Gesellschaft* regional church that serves people from a twenty- or thirty-mile radius.

The methodology employed in the process of launching a new mission can have a powerful impact on the future identity of that worshiping community.

Is the methodology you use compatible with the identity you are seeking to create for this new mission? Are you planning a community- or neighborhood-based mission or for a commuter clientele?

Place and Identity?

"We purchased a three-acre parcel for this new church next door to the proposed new elementary school in this subdivision," explained a denominational leader. "We want this new mission to be identified with family life, children, and this neighborhood."

* * *

"We were fortunate that more than a hundred years ago when the old building burned, the leaders of that day chose this corner

121

for the new building. Today we are at the heart of the central business district," reflected the senior pastor of a thriving downtown church. "Our location is ideal for a downtown ministry."

* * *

"We were given this site by the developer who is a member of our congregation. He wouldn't sell any land for church sites within that retirement community, but he gave us these seven acres directly across the street from the only entrance into that fenced-in community of over two thousand dwelling units. Whenever anyone drives out of there, all they have to do is wait for the green light and drive across the highway into our parking lot. Those residents tend to identify this as their church because of our proximity, but because we are across the street we also have an appeal to the rest of the folks around here," boasted the pastor of this nine-year-old congregation. "We have the best of both worlds. We're convenient to four thousand retirees, but we're not solely identified with that community."

* * *

"My father-in-law designed this building, and my wife and I put in literally hundreds of hours helping construct it six years ago," recalled a charter member of a six-year-old congregation. "When the new pastor suggested we relocate because he doesn't think two acres is sufficient for a new church, my wife and I were among the majority that voted down the recommendation to relocate. We have too much of ourselves invested in this place to sell it to another church and start all over again at some other location."

These four comments illustrate the fact that for many people the identity of a congregation is closely tied with that meeting place. How much weight do you give this as you create a list of criteria for the selection of a permanent meeting place?

The Organizational Life

"Our chancel choir director is one of the finest examples of a committed Christian I've ever met. Our chancel choir is first of all a closely knit and supportive religious community. The second part of our choir's identity is in rehearsing and singing an anthem every

Sunday," explained the pastor of a four-year-old mission. "We also have a strong men's fellowship, a great women's organization, an outstanding youth group, and a big Sunday school. The last time I checked, three-quarters of our recent new members came into this church through one of those five organizations. The church I served before I took this assignment was built around a network of strong organizations and I decided that would be the model I would follow when I accepted this assignment. I've seen too many new missions lose half their members when that magnetic personality who was the organizing pastor left.

"Instead of building this congregation around me," continued this forty-seven-year-old pastor, "I wanted something that would last, and I'm convinced this is it. I'm proud to say that no one dropped out of either of the two churches I served earlier after I left. I tried to help every person identify with and be a loyal member of one of the organizations rather than simply be loyal to me. Too often a lot of church members identify with the preacher rather than with that worshiping community. I don't believe in that! Of course, I have a lot of close friends here in this congregation and I know some of the charter members joined because they liked me or they were favorably impressed with my preaching or they found that first worship service they shared in to be a meaningful experience. That is a natural part of that first chapter in a new congregation. As soon as I could, however, I began to build the organizational life. The first step was the Sunday school. One of my goals was to enhance the attractiveness of our children's division. I wanted a Sunday school that was so good that the six-year-old or the twelve-year-old who came for the first time would demand of their parents that they come back here next Sunday. I also wanted a strong adult division so the adults would want to return.

"The second was the men's fellowship. The third was the choir. That should have been first, but it took several months for me to find the person I was seeking to direct it. The fourth was the junior high youth group. The next was a senior youth group. In both of those I held off until I could find the type of adult volunteers we needed. The last was our women's organization. That came last because many of our early volunteers were busy helping create the rest of the organizational life.

IT CAN BE ADDED TO WITHOUT UPSETTING ITS BALANCE!

CHANCEL CHOIR
MEN'S FELLOWSHIP
SUNDAY SCHOOL
ADULT DIVISION
JUNIOR HIGH GROUP
WOMEN'S SUMMER MISSION PROJECT
SENIOR HIGH GROUP
—FRIAR TUCK

For growth & assimilation, new churches need to be, congregations of congregations!

"Today this is a congregation, not of three hundred confirmed members, but rather a congregation of congregations. Each organization is a mini-congregation. Each one is a lay-owned, lay-operated, self-governing, self-financing, and self-propagating body of Christians. Each organization is an attractive entry point for new members. Each organization also is responsible for the assimilation of new people and the care of its members. Of course, we have some people who come who don't want to belong to any of these organizations, but as I told you earlier, about three-quarters of our recent new members came in through one of these organizations. This congregation already is too large for most people to identify with it, and I expect we'll at least triple in size before our tenth birthday. We can do that by expanding the organizational life."

A persuasive argument can be made that this is the best model for new church development. It probably is the second best model, next to building around excellent biblical preaching, but these two models are not mutually incompatible. The organizational life provides a varied network of entry points for new members. One of the natural attributes of most organizations is to develop its own distinctive identity. Each one naturally tends to facilitate the assimilation of new people. This model of congregational life not only depends heavily on lay volunteers, it also can nurture the personal and spiritual journey of those lay volunteers. It challenges the laity to be active leaders rather than passive spectators or critics. The stronger the organizational life, the less the dependence on paid program staff. Since most members identify with their favorite organization, rather than with the minister, the departure of that pastor who planted that new church usually is not as disruptive as it is when the mission is built around the personality and/or the pulpit ability of the mission-developer minister.

If this is such a wonderful model, why is it not used more widely?

Perhaps the number-one reason is that few ministers have the skills, the vision, the experience, the professional and personal security and self-confidence, the personality, and the gifts required to make this approach to ministry work.

Second, it requires a sensitive denominational support

WE COULD PERISH IF WE REFUSE to MAKE THE WORLD OUR PARISH!

The difference between GEMEINSCHAFT and GESELLSCHAFT is as clear as dying and growing!
—FRIAR TUCK

system that places a high priority on strengthening and resourcing the organizational life of congregations. Too often the regional judicatories or national agencies have their own agenda that they want to advance. This may cause them to see congregations as potential allies in advancing that denominational agenda, rather than as institutions in need of support and nurture. This model requires that the first priority for the regional and national agencies must be the agendas of congregations. That may be an unrealistic expectation to place on any long-established institution in American society today.

Third, and some will argue this is the critical factor, this model is based on the assumption that when challenged with a vision and granted the opportunity to display their gifts and skills, the laity will respond with creativity, energy, dedication, and hard work. Not everyone believes that.

Fourth, this approach is incompatible with the dependency model of new church development used by several denominations which includes large initial financial subsidies, centralized policy making, continuing financial support, a requirement for outside approval of local decisions, and continued oversight.

125

That model of new church development tends to repel those adults who would be the most effective volunteers in creating a congregation that is a collection of lay-owned, lay-controlled, self-governing, self-financing, and self-propagating organizations. That dependency model also rarely attracts as mission developers pastors who are comfortable with the idea of centering much of the identity in the organizational life. In today's world this model of new church development will be encountered most often in independent churches or in congregations affiliated with a denomination with a history of congregational autonomy.

Finally, many ministers may object to this model because of two misgivings. First, it may minimize the centrality of the Word, of the sacraments, and of the confessions. Second, it is vulnerable to the tail-wags-the-dog syndrome. Without strong pastoral oversight, some organizations may become exceptionally powerful and begin to lead an independent life rather than obey Saint Paul's plea for interdependence. This may be most visible in the parish elementary school, but it also has been seen in the Sunday school, the women's organization, the choir, the men's fellowship, and the youth group. Unless the pastor is comfortable living with and reducing that risk, this can be a threatening model.

As you develop a strategy for new church development, are you willing to encourage strengthening the identity and role of the organizational life of a new mission?

New Becomes Old

Perhaps the most subtle threat to the identity of a new mission is the passage of time. The glamour, the sense of adventure, the attraction of helping pioneer the new, and the challenge to be part of an exciting new creation are unique assets of the new mission. It can be completely oriented toward tomorrow. The past, tradition, custom, and yesterday have little weight in making policy decisions. A part of the distinctive identity of that mission is in that wonderful and attractive word "new." It parallels the power of that term when placed ahead of such mundane words as "baby," "house," "car," "job," "husband," "wife," or "pet."

When does the new become old? When does the identity of that new congregation have to shift from new to what it is today?

One answer is when the sponsoring denomination launches a newer church in that community. Another is when the original pastor is replaced by a successor. A third is when the charter membership roll is closed. A fourth is when the congregation moves from a temporary to a permanent meeting place. A fifth is when many of the original volunteer leaders have left. A sixth is when financial, real estate, and other institutional needs replace evangelism at the top of the agenda. A seventh is when the pastor suddenly discovers "I'm devoting more time to the care of our current members than I am to meeting and enlisting future members." An eighth is about five to eight years after that first worship service was held. A ninth is when the past and tradition replace the future and creativity in planning the calendar for the coming year. A tenth is when a newer congregation now exceeds this one in size.

At this point the question arises, If our identity no longer is in being a *new* mission, what is it? Is it in the personality of our pastor? In our denominational label? In our program? In our position on the theological spectrum? In our charter members? In our organizational life? In our size? In our location and meeting place? In our relationships with other churches? In our community image? (If so, what is it? Has it changed?) In our recent new members? In our *new* pastor? In community service programs?

The two bad answers to that question are (1) we don't have a distinctive identity or (2) we're quarreling over the definition of our identity. The second repels prospective new members. The first tends to minimize the capability to attract additional new members.

Who determines the identity in what until recently was a *new* mission? What will be the criteria in making that decision? Have you discussed the probable implications of that decision with your volunteer leaders?

CHAPTER ELEVEN

Those Pioneer Volunteer Leaders

From a long-term perspective one of the most significant decisions in planting a new church is the choice of that initial cadre of volunteer leaders. A review of the experiences of new congregations reveals a huge array of alternative approaches for enlisting that initial cadre of volunteer leaders. Perhaps the worst approach is to bless every person who comes along and volunteers to be a leader. The second worst is the traditional search for warm bodies to fill vacant slots in the organizational table.

A far better approach is to seek volunteer leaders in a manner that is consistent with the vision behind the launching of this congregation. (See chapter 2.)

If the vision calls for creating a carbon copy or clone of the sponsoring church as part of a strategy to limit the growth of that mother church, it may be wise to enlist five or six volunteers from the central core of the lay leadership of that sponsoring church. The achievement of this goal often will be facilitated if the pastor or a long-tenured associate minister of that sponsoring church is the founding pastor of the new mission. In scores of cases this strategy has been effective in diverting two-thirds or more of what might have been future members of the sponsoring church to that new mission meeting in a newer building at a larger and more attractive site a couple of miles away.

If the vision calls for building the identity of the new mission in a comprehensive collection of lay-owned and lay-operated organizations (see chapter 10), such as a strong Sunday school, an attractive ministry of music, a vigorous men's fellowship, a vital women's organization, and a dynamic youth program, it may help to maximize the number of lay volunteer leaders who come from the ranks of the self-employed. These include farmers, persons who own and operate their own business, homemakers, independent contractors, and classroom teachers. If this is the vision driving that new mission, it may be wise to minimize the number of volunteer leaders who are middle-level employees in a large bureaucratic structure and maximize the number of venturesome, risk-taking, creative, and entrepreneurial personalities.

HI! HOW WOULD YOU LIKE to BE A VOLUNTEER LEADER?

The self-employed make the best leaders in churches seeking to be self-dependent!
—FRIAR TUCK

If the vision is to build a new mission to reach the unchurched, it may be wise to spend several months evangelizing among people who have had no active relationships with any worshiping community for many years followed by an overlapping period of discipling these new Christians before they are asked to accept volunteer leadership responsibilities.

If the new mission is composed largely of "displaced people" (see chapter 10) who have moved here for economic reasons, it often is possible to enlist a cadre of volunteer leaders from among those who carried similar responsibilities in another congregation before moving here.

If this is a new mission to reach and serve recent immigrants from another country, it may be wise to be especially sensitive to an already defined deference pyramid before enlisting volunteer leaders.

If this new mission is designed to reach residents of a retirement community, it may be useful to look first at the dynamics of that type of community before beginning that search for volunteer leaders. Frequently, mature adults moving to another state to retire prefer volunteer assignments that include precisely stated rules, boundaries, expectations, and a firm terminal date. For others a volunteer leadership responsibility can become a great challenge to their creativity.[1]

If this new mission is designed to reach and serve adults who were reared in the Roman Catholic Church and their religious pilgrimage brings them to a new Protestant mission, it may be wise to offer an extensive orientation course for prospective future members (and perhaps for recent new members) before beginning that search for volunteer leaders. A thorough orientation program can prevent future misunderstandings.

If the vision calls for creating a large, multi-faceted regional church with a thousand or more members, it may be wise to enlist several volunteer leaders who have held policy-making positions in other very large churches and who thus understand some of the distinctive characteristics of the large congregation.[2] It also helps if several of these volunteers are comfortable with a strategy that includes quantified numerical goals.

If the vision calls for creating a new congregation built around a network of one-to-one relationships with the pastor at the hub of that network,[3] it may be wise to enlist several volunteer leaders early who are (1) strong, personal supporters of the pastor, (2) gregarious, extroverted, warm, loving, outgoing, and neighbor-centered individuals, and (3) more interested in people than in program.

If the vision calls for a short-tenured church planter who will move to start another new mission after only a few years, that initial volunteer cadre should include at least a half-dozen task-oriented adults who possess skills in institution building and who place a high value on taking care of administrative details on time.

If the goal is to create a financially self-supporting congregation within twelve to eighteen months, the mission-developer pastor should be a minister who believes in tithing, is a tither, is comfortable talking about tithing, is convinced that a commitment to tithing is a prerequisite to becoming a volunteer leader in that new mission, and is comfortable with the role of "money raiser." Modeling is a most powerful pedagogical technique in human society. If, however, the new mission is organized on a dependency model with an expectation of long-term denominational subsidies, this may be an unimportant consideration.

If the central organizing principle is to build this new mission around a powerful teaching ministry, at least one-half of the volunteer policy makers should be adults who already have accepted a teaching assignment in that new congregation and are fulfilling that responsibility effectively.

If the vision calls for combining a new worshiping community with a new Christian day school, all of the volunteer leaders should be drawn from among those who are committed proponents of the private, avowedly Christian day school.

If the goal is to reach and serve the generations born after 1955, at least 70 percent of all volunteer policy makers should be drawn from among those born after 1955.

If a major goal is to reach adults who are seeking a new church home following remarriage, at least 40 percent of the volunteer policy makers should be persons in their second or subsequent marriage.

If the vision calls for creating a high demand church (see chapter 10), all volunteer leaders should be drawn from among those who participate in corporate worship at least twice weekly, are tithers, are committed participants in a continuing adult Bible study group, and also carry other volunteer responsibilities.

If one of the goals is to reach and serve that growing number of parents who prefer to teach their children at home rather than enroll them in a public or private school, at least one-fourth of the volunteer policy makers should be home schoolers.

WITHOUT A VISION, THE PEOPLE PERISH!

...without volunteers who match that vision many a new mission never becomes a parish!
—FRIAR TUCK

WHAT "GRABS ME" IS WHOEVER IS OUT TO GET ME!

Our identity and vision are determined by the objects of our outreach!
—FRIAR TUCK

These examples are offered to illustrate the concept that the criteria for the selection of that initial cadre of volunteer policy makers should be consistent with and supportive of the vision and goals.

For those who are both reading and counting sequentially, this is number thirty on this list of 44 questions, but the criteria used in the selection of those first volunteer leaders ranks among the half-dozen most far-reaching decisions a church planter will make.

CHAPTER TWELVE

The Place of Missions

Overlapping the significance of an intentionally designed set of criteria for the selection of those initial volunteer leaders is another critical question. What will be the place of missions in this new church?

A tempting response is to see this new congregation as "mission." It is easy for the pioneers in a new church to persuade themselves, "We are the expression of the missionary outreach of the church." This tempts people to justify devoting all available resources to making this a successful venture. Every minute of volunteer time, every dollar in the offering plate, and every bit of energy of the pastor should be directed to strengthening this fragile new creation. "Later on, when we have discretionary resources, we can become supportive of the worldwide missionary outreach of the Christian Church."

That is bad theology that creates a bad precedent and is inconsistent with the New Testament.

From both a biblical perspective and a pragmatic stance a better approach is to make missions a central facet of the vision from day one. This is especially important if the primary focus in the evangelistic outreach is to be on (a) adults who have never made a profession of faith or even accepted Jesus Christ as Lord and Savior, they need to be instructed in the centrality of missions in the Christian faith, or (b) families with young children, those children will gain their first understanding of the Christian faith from their experiences in this new mission, or (c) churchgoing adults moving here from another community, many of whom will be attracted by a church that places a high value on missions, and they all need to have the central place of missions reaffirmed, or (d) disillusioned former churchgoers who have dropped out of church, the most effective way to overcome their disillusionment and cynicism is to place missions at the heart of the vision, or (e)

133

SOONER OR LATER, SUCH A CHURCH IS GONNA GETCHA!

Evangelism and mission tend to be the marks of new churches!

—FRIAR TUCK

mature adults who have moved here in their retirement years, many of whom were taught the importance of missions in the first several decades of life and will be impressed by an emphasis on missions, or (f) the generations born between 1930 and 1955 who were influenced by the rebellious era of the 1960s, many of them became convinced that missions and social action are the primary tasks of every worshiping community, or (g) that growing number of religious pilgrims who see themselves on a faith journey without a clearly defined destination, they can be challenged by the church that sees itself as concerned about *both* individual salvation *and* the needs of today's world, or (h) single adults who are shaping and reshaping their personal faith and need help in keeping missions and outreach at the heart of that personal faith, or (i) building an inclusive community of people from a variety of racial, ethnic, economic, nationality, occupational, and social backgrounds, the best unifying point for such a group of people is missions—and also a way of minimizing navel-gazing and self-congratulatory programming, or (j) people who have no first-hand knowledge of our denominational heritage, missions is a better bridge than doctrine, polity, history, or tradition in reaching across denominational and faith barriers, or (k) teenagers and families with teenagers, active involvement in missions is the most effective single entry point into today's "adolescent society," or (l) immigrants from another country, an emphasis on missions can be a rallying point, a link with the mother country, and a tie with other congregations composed of the same nationality group, or (m) people who come seeking only to have their own bucket of religious needs filled, they need to understand Jesus gave us two great commandments, not one.

How this emphasis on missions will be expressed will vary. A common pattern is the announcement at that first worship service that beginning with today the first 10 or 15 percent of all offerings will go for missions. Another is to build mission education into the study program. A third entry point for future new members is that of annual mission work camp experience. A fourth is to tithe the building fund to help an overseas church. A fifth is to enlist volunteers to work in the local program for sheltering the homeless or feeding the hungry or visiting those in jail. A sixth is to create an adult day care program. A seventh is to build one group or organization around that focus on missions. An eighth is to adopt a "sister church" on another continent and reinforce that relationship with annual exchanges of members for a week or two. A ninth is to challenge members to accept a call to serve as a missionary. A tenth is to help sponsor another new mission.

How will the centrality of missions be expressed in your new church?

CHAPTER THIRTEEN

Six Questions on Real Estate and Finances

"The idiot who purchased this site simply didn't know what he was doing, and this congregation has been handicapped for its entire life by the limitations of this piece of property," angrily explained the fifth pastor in the life of this thirty-nine-year-old congregation. "It's too small, it's almost impossible for strangers to find, and a third of it is so steep all it's good for is landscaping. About the only good thing about it is that it cost less than $3,000 when they bought it."

* * *

"We figure before we're through, every new church we organize will cost us between $250,000 and $600,000," declared a denominational executive responsible for new church development. "We make a grant to cover all operating expenses the first year and one-half of the second and third year's expenses. In addition, we give every new congregation a paid-for parcel of land and sometimes we subsidize the interest rate on a second mortgage on that first unit."

* * *

"We have new missions we've been subsidizing for over twenty years, and we don't know how to get them off the dole," wearily complained another executive.

* * *

"Our biggest problem is how to finance our second unit," reflected the pastor of a four-year-old mission in a perplexed tone of voice. "The week we moved into our first building a year ago, we were crowded. We need a second unit in order to continue to grow, but we can't build it because we still owe $400,000 on this first unit."

Comments such as these illustrate some of the many questions on real estate and finances confronting those responsible for new church development and those who have to live with the consequences of the answers to these questions.

The Initial Financing

For many the biggest question is the amount and the sources of the initial financial support of the pastor or the staff team that will organize that new mission. The answer usually has long-term implications and often shapes the future culture of that congregation. The range of possibilities can be illustrated by looking at a half-dozen models.

At one end of this spectrum is the venturesome, self-confident, and optimistic individual who is driven by what is perceived as a divine call from God to go out and create a new Christian congregation. Frequently, this venture is financed by a secular job on the side, sometimes out of savings, and for others, out of the earnings of an employed spouse. This is clearly the most widely used approach to the initial financing of a new congregation in the United States today. It is especially common in the creation of new African-American, Spanish language, Asian, and working class churches.

At the other end of this spectrum is the rarest approach. This is when a denominational entity guarantees the mission-developer pastor a full compensation package including salary, housing, health insurance, pension payments, and other benefits for a year or two or three. Sometimes that also includes a grant for the purchase of a parcel of land, and it may even include a grant or

137

below market interest rate loan for construction of the first building. These high costs mean the number of new churches to receive this initial financing must be a modest total.

This high front-end cost is used most often by those seeking to reach upper-middle and upper income Anglos who are comfortable with institutional subsidies. Occasionally this approach also is followed by predominantly Anglo denominations seeking to reach segments of the ethnic and minority population. It is justified on egalitarian principles that require equal subsidies regardless of race, language, income, or social class. A common result is to enhance the dependency syndrome and create small and economically dependent congregations.

Another rarely used approach has been to place a limit on the initial subsidy by a one-time financial grant. Typically this is in the $35,000 to $75,000 bracket. It is based on two assumptions. First, continuing financial subsidies usually are injurious to the spiritual and institutional health of congregations. Second, somewhere out there is an entrepreneurial minister who will accept the challenge to launch a new congregation and agrees that all that is required is a financial subsidy for several months to cover the initial costs for compensation, program, publicity, and rental of a temporary meeting place. It is assumed that within several months this should, can, and will become a self-financing, self-propagating, and self-governing congregation.

This relatively low cost model is receiving increasing attention, but tends not to arouse support from those who (a) prefer a dependency model, or (b) believe $75,000 is an excessively large initial grant, or (c) are convinced a minimum subsidy of $250,000 is required for every new church, or (d) know no minister would accept that challenge, or (e) know it is impossible for any new congregation to be able to finance its own capital costs.

A more common model is for a sponsoring church to guarantee the full compensation of the church planter for the first twelve to eighteen months, for a second sponsoring congregation to guarantee either the compensation of a second staff person and/or basic program costs for twelve to eighteen months, and for several other congregations together to finance the purchase of a parcel of land for that permanent meeting place.

Among the advantages of this model are (1) it is easier to raise money for that new church development when the financial grants go directly to the recipient mission rather than through a denominational agency, (2) that twelve- or eighteen- or twenty-four-month terminal date for subsidies is clearly defined and extremely difficult to extend, (3) it satisfies the evangelistic imperative for the sponsoring churches to help launch new congregations without getting involved in the complexities that often accompany sending out a nucleus of charter members, (4) it enables a church in Texas to sponsor a new mission in Minnesota or a congregation in Iowa to sponsor a new church in Arkansas, (5) it encourages the creation of a new mission that is the "daughter" of *several* parent congregations, (6) this joint sponsorship can encourage accountability that does not take the form of control, and (7) it encourages the mission-developer pastor and that initial cadre of volunteer leaders to accept the need to become financially self-supporting.

A fifth model is for a denominational entity to purchase the land for a permanent meeting place many years in advance while costs are still modest, to decide when the time is ripe, and to offer an initial financial subsidy that might cover three-fourths of operating expenses the first year, one-half the second year, and one-quarter the third year.

A sixth model is for a long-established congregation to sell its property, relocate, and use that accumulated capital to finance the cost of land and buildings for a new start at a new location for a new tomorrow. A less common variation of this is for three or four small congregations to agree to merge, to sell their assets, pool that money, purchase a new site at a new location, and construct a new building under a new name with new ministerial leadership committed to turning that dream into a new tomorrow.

These examples are intended only to illustrate the range of possibilities, not to suggest that only six alternatives exist. Three key critical generalizations to come out of recent experiences are instructive.

A. Large long-term financial subsidies tend to encourage dependency and discourage numerical growth.

B. The sources and amount of that initial financing can be the most significant factor in screening that list of candidates to be church planters. The larger the financial guarantee, the smaller

139

the number of candidates who will withdraw their candidacy. The smaller the promised subsidy, the more likely the most competent candidates will seek that challenge.

C. If the goal is to raise large sums of money to sponsor a large number of new churches, this is more likely to be accomplished if (1) individuals are challenged to contribute directly to specific new missions for capital expenditures, (2) a good system of accountability and feedback makes it easy for contributors to know what happened as a result of their gifts, (3) congregations are challenged to sponsor mission developers by providing that person's compensation for a stated period of time and they receive accurate information for accountability and evaluation as well as to encourage direct grants for capital improvements, and (4) the denominational entity responsible for new church development concentrates its efforts and resources on (a) advance acquisition of land, (b) recruiting, screening, training, and placing church planters, (c) enlisting sponsoring or "partner" individuals and churches to make short-term direct grants or loans, (d) never offering any financial subsidy, either direct or indirect, to any new mission—that can become addictive for both parties, (e) providing expert consultation services to new missions on stewardship, evangelism, architectural design, and education as well as leadership development events for lay and clergy leaders, (f) creating and operating a revolving fund from which congregations can borrow money at market level interest rates for construction (this usually is an ecclesiastical version of the traditional savings and loan association), and (g) accepting the responsibility for deciding when new missions will be started and where they will be located.

In several denominations the polity means this must be a cooperative venture between a regional judicatory and/or a cluster of nearby congregations and a national agency. One of the reasons the independent or nondenominational churches have been so effective in recent years in launching new congregations is that each has a highly centralized system that avoids this need for interagency cooperation and also eliminates the blight of NIMBY. (When long-established churches veto proposals to start a new mission nearby by protesting Not in My Back Yard!)

What is your strategy for mobilizing that initial financing?

140

Financing That First Building

Four pressures often cause the new mission to plateau with fewer than one hundred fifty people at worship. The first and the most subtle is to begin with a relatively small number of people who soon cause the new mission to focus inwardly. As that happens, it is easy for the pioneers to agree, "We simply do not have the resources necessary to build our own meeting place!"

This often produces a delay in moving out of that rented temporary meeting place into permanent quarters.

All too often it turns out in retrospect that the evangelistic capability of a new mission begins to erode after meeting for about three or four years in that first temporary meeting place. This reinforces the reluctance to venture forth in a building program.

The second pressure has been mentioned earlier. This is to build that new congregation as a network of one-to-one relationships with the pastor at the hub. Unless this pastor is an exceptionally productive worker and excels in time management, this model usually means the new congregation continues to meet in temporary quarters

SINCE WE'RE IN the 'SPIRIT-BUSINESS" WE NEED LITTLE ELSE!

—FRIAR TUCK·

The less we make our church plantings dependent upon substidy, the more dependable they'll be!

ALAS, A SUBSTIDY CAN PRODUCE APATHY!

Direct or indirect financial aid can be addictive to both the givers and receivers!

—FRIAR TUCK·

141

year after year. The leaders feel their numbers are too small to undertake a major construction program so they continue in rented quarters. Sometimes the denomination offers a very large subsidy to encourage construction of that first unit without recognizing that heavily subsidized missions following that approach to ministry now have two reasons not to grow. One is that one-to-one style of ministry. The second is the denominational subsidy.

The third pressure is to secure an architect who will produce a "master plan" of what this congregation will need in new permanent buildings by year twenty-five in its history. The cost of this often is intimidating and/or immobilizing.

The fourth pressure is the rarely questioned assumption in upper-middle and upper income communities that the first building at the first location will be the first unit of a permanent facility at that location. (By contrast, most African-American, Hispanic, Asian, and Anglo working class new missions assume their pilgrimage will take them from modest rented temporary quarters to larger rented quarters to a temporary meeting place that they will own as part of their journey to their "permanent" church home.)

The best way to avoid the problems produced by these pressures is to begin with a nucleus of at least a couple hundred worshipers.

An alternative is to purchase a "secondhand" building as the first-owned meeting place. While this has risks, the risks usually are not as serious as remaining in rented facilities for longer than three years. (A fourth year in rented facilities can be acceptable if by the beginning of that fourth year it is universally understood that this new meeting place soon will be available.)

One of the most creative alternatives has been suggested by a couple of leaders in the United Church of Christ. This calls for the new mission to construct a new one-story building in an industrial park with the expectation that property subsequently will be sold for commercial uses. This alternative assumes (a) the vision behind the launching of that new mission calls for this to become a very large congregation, therefore the location of that temporary meeting place is not important, (b) the financial restrictions on the new mission mean it cannot afford a 15,000 to 20,000 square foot conventional church building, (c) this type of construction costs about one-third to one-half as much per square foot as the conventional church building so the tradeoff is more space for less money, but at a temporary location, (d) the industrial park is located on or near a major highway so it will be easily accessible, (e) continued inflation means the new mission probably can sell this property for more than it has invested in it, (f) a permanent site can and will be purchased as a long-term alternative location, but this is not essential at this stage, (g) the local municipality will grant the new mission permission to meet in the industrial park for a stated period of time, (h) the development authority owning the industrial park will recognize the benefits of this proposal, (i) the target audience for this new mission is a drive-in, not a walk-in congregation, and (j) the leaders of the new mission will affirm the merits of this tradeoff.

Among the advantages of this model are (1) the new mission gains the benefits of being able to meet in a very large building designed for religious uses, (2) a one-story design, (3) an abundance of off-street parking for evenings and Sundays, (4) adequate space for seven-day-a-week programming, (5) flexibility to wait until the distinctive identity of this congregation has emerged before making a commitment to a particular location or a specific building design, (6) an opportunity for daytime ministries with people employed in that industrial park, (7) avoidance of a distinctive social class identity that often is a product of being located in a residential neighborhood, and (8) the satisfactions that go with "meeting in our own place" versus being a tenant.

Another alternative is to design that first unit as "light construction," that resembles a residence rather than a school or a hospital. This can cut the costs per square foot by 50 percent, but the tradeoff is maintenance costs will be higher. One of the big advantages of light construction, however, is it is more amenable to the use of volunteer work crews. In several denominations most of the labor for that first unit is contributed by volunteers from other churches. This alternative can produce a 15,000 square foot structure for the dollar outlay required for the 5,000 square foot heavy construction first unit built by a contractor.

A fifth alternative is to utilize low cost factory-manufactured buildings on what is assumed will be "our permanent site." One advantage of this is the relatively low cost. A second is the early

OF COURSE, IT DOESN'T FEEL LIKE HOME, BUT IT IS "HOMEWARD-BOUND"!

Temporary structures are both economical and motivational "first-homes" for new missions!
—FRIAR TUCK

identification with that site and location. A third is that this can be a pragmatic test of the merits of that location and site before investing large sums in permanent facilities. Several congregations have discovered after a year or two that this really is a poor location and/or the site is inadequate and/or limitations exist that were not foreseen when the land was purchased.

A significant advantage is the comparatively low cost of these buildings enables the new mission to move out of that temporary rented facility very early and to begin to grow in numbers, and that growth in numbers and programming creates the discontent that facilitates the construction of permanent facilities.

Perhaps the most obvious advantage of either light construction with volunteer crews or a factory-built first unit is that the congregation can exploit the benefits of meeting at the same location in those low cost buildings while construction of that permanent first unit is underway. In other words, the new mission can gain the benefits of a "permanent place" long before it is able to finance the construction of permanent facilities. The importance of place in people's lives is one of the themes of the Old Testament, it is a major thread in the history of African-American churches, it is a powerful factor in the life expectancy of mature adults, and it is largely ignored by policy makers in the churches.[1]

The biggest argument against the use of manufactured buildings as the first meeting place at that permanent location is that many municipalities place severe restrictions on this alternative.

The second biggest argument against these buildings is that

they may be so comfortable, compared to the rented facilities used for the first several months, that the resulting absence of discontent makes it difficult to motivate people to tackle a construction program. One means of offsetting this risk is to obtain a temporary use permit from the unit of local government. A second is for the denomination to own these manufactured buildings and to rent them to the new mission with a clear understanding that the rent increases by $25 or $50 every month. Thus the rent the first month might be $100, but in month thirty-seven it would be $1,000. Do not underestimate the power of economic motivation!

While the benefits of being able to move into that first congregationally owned meeting house are many, the risks of premature action should not be overlooked. One risk is that financial limitations or an extravagant design will produce a first unit that is so small it limits growth. A second is the new mission may overestimate future growth and agree to a debt service schedule that turns out to be oppressive when that growth does not materialize. This can lead to a campaign to enlist more members for reasons of institutional survival rather than for proclamation of the gospel. It also may lead to the premature departure of the founding pastor. A third risk is that the growth exceeds expectations and that first unit is too small from day one, but the financial obligations are too great to allow expansion.

Instead of setting a goal to be in that first unit before the end of the third or fourth year, it may be wise to turn from the calendar to quantifiable goals or mileposts. For example, a reasonable way to state this would be construction should not begin until after (1) the average attendance at worship exceeds 175 for three consecutive months, (2) the number of names on the list of prospective new members approaches two hundred, (3) the building fund contains at least $100,000 in cash and invested receipts, (4) five thousand calls have been completed on individual householders, and (5) two hundred people have united with this new mission during the past twelve months. In some cases a construction program can be justified if at least three of these five conditions have been met. These milepost goals tend to encourage activity while calendar goals ("We will begin construction in year three") may encourage passivity.

NOW...WHAT DO I HEAR FOR THE NEXT TON of BRICKS?

NEW CHURCH AUCTION

Another financial appeal while building can be most productive!

— FRIAR TUCK

Land costs vary so greatly and the means of financing the cost of that permanent site takes so many different forms, it is impossible to offer suggestions that will fit all situations.

Among the more common alternatives are these twelve: (1) a systematic advance site acquisition by the denomination that purchases land for new churches many years in advance and those sites subsequently are made available to new missions or "traded" for what have turned out to be superior sites, (2) one or more sponsoring churches fund all or part of the costs, (3) an individual benefactor gives the new mission the property, (4) the new mission identifies and purchases its own site for a permanent meeting place, (5) the new mission purchases the land and buildings of an existing congregation that is relocating, (6) a denominational agency purchases the property and conveys it to the new mission with a reversionary clause in the contract, (7) the new mission purchases a school building, an office structure, a warehouse, a new car retailer's property, or some other property on the open market and remodels it for religious uses, (8) the new mission purchases a large parcel of land and a few years later sells part of it to help pay for construction of a building, (9) the new mission purchases (or is given) a site which subsequently it sells to purchase another site at a more appropriate location, (10) one or more sponsoring churches loan the money for site acquisition on a second mortgage so the new mission can take out a first mortgage from a commercial lending institution for construction of that first building, (11) a sponsoring church finances site acquisition costs with a very low interest rate second mortgage with the stipulation that mortgage will be canceled when the new mission purchases a site for some other new mission and/or the interest rate on that second mortgage rises by 1

GULP! THIS ISN'T the WIDOW'S MITE BUT THE OFFERING of OUR LARGEST GIVER!

A short-term capital funds appeal will give a clearer estimate of commitment than any congregational vote!

—FRIAR TUCK.

percentage point every twelve months, (12) a "church builder's club" of committed individuals provides the money to purchase sites for new missions.

Likewise a variety of means are being used to finance the costs of that first building. An increasingly common practice is based on the assumption that (a) giving is habit forming and (b) the typical individual will make a larger contribution the second time than the first. Thus a twelve-month capital funds appeal covering two consecutive tax years is organized and completed during the planning stages for that new building. A second one-hundred-week or a one-hundred-fifty-week capital funds appeal follows that to coincide with the actual construction of that first unit. Among the advantages of this two-stage approach are (1) the availability of capital funds to pay early costs rather than borrowing and paying interest, (2) that first appeal is a useful "practice" effort, (3) the second appeal raises far more money than the first, partly because it is longer, partly because it usually includes more contributors, partly because it coincides with the actual construction, and partly because second appeals usually produce more money per month per contributor than do first appeals (giving is habit forming plus practice), (4) the first appeal can be designed to reach accumulated wealth (savings) while the second appeal may be designed primarily to reach current income, and (5) that first appeal can be the most meaningful available means of determining the degree of support for going into a construction program at this time. It usually is far more reflective of reality than a secret congregational vote or an open discussion at a big congregational meeting.

In some churches the required congregational vote on a building program is scheduled to follow after that first capital funds appeal.

The results of that appeal provide useful factual data for those who will cast a ballot on that issue. One of the misleading characteristics of that secret ballot at a congregational meeting is that the votes of those four fringe members who rarely attend worship, who are strongly opposed to constructing that proposed new building at this time, and who probably will not contribute a dime to the cost are given twice the weight of the two affirmative votes cast by that loyal couple who never miss church, who are enthusiastic volunteers, and who may contribute $100,000 to the building fund. Participatory decision-making requires giving everyone a voice, but it does not require counting all votes as equal! This is one reason for scheduling a short-term capital funds appeal ahead of a congregational vote on constructing a new building.

Typically, a first mortgage is used to borrow the remaining costs of the construction of that first unit. In an increasing number of new missions the rapid increase in construction costs plus the expensive requirements of the municipal building code plus the need today for more space for the same number of people than was required in 1950[2] mean supplemental financing will be required. The financial capability of that new congregation today often is not sufficient to meet the capital costs through the combination of a building fund campaign and a commercial loan.

One alternative is to sell bonds to members of other churches or on the open market. (For reasons too complicated to elaborate on here, it should be clearly stated this alternative is NOT recommended by this writer!)

A second is for a sponsoring church to offer a second mortgage with a zero interest rate the first year, an interest rate of 1 percent the second year, 2 percent the third year, and 3 percent the fourth year that continues to rise by 1 percentage point annually until the new mission feels it would be economically wise to pay off that second mortgage.

A third is for a sponsoring church's mission foundation to contribute one dollar for every two dollars the new mission raises in that first capital funds appeal. The matching grant concept can be a powerful motivating force!

A fourth is a second mortgage from that denominational revolving loan fund for new churches.

A fifth is the church builders club of individuals who contribute $100 to $2,500 each to the building fund of every new mission.

A sixth is that team of volunteers from the regional judicatory of that denomination who give two to ten weeks every year to serve on a well-managed construction crew. This crew comes in and provides most of the labor required for construction of new church buildings. Many of these volunteers are committed Christians who are loyal members of that denomination, have chosen early retirement, and enjoy this opportunity to express their love of the Lord through volunteer service.

A seventh is to seek major memorial gifts for specific rooms, furnishings, and fixtures.

An eighth is for a denominational entity to subsidize part of the cost of that new building either by outright grants or by a below-market level interest rate on a mortgage.

A ninth is to postpone construction to coincide with the third capital funds drive rather than the second campaign.

A tenth, as mentioned earlier, is to purchase a secondhand church building and postpone construction of that new permanent building.

That Second Building

A common price tag on rapid growth in a new mission was illustrated in the fourth paragraph of this chapter. That first unit is crowded when it is completed, but the size of the mortgage and debt service payments make it impossible to undertake construction of the needed additional space. What can be done?

One alternative is patience. A second is the rental of temporary space off campus. A third is for classes to meet in the homes of nearby members. A fourth is the use of low cost manufactured structures on campus. A fifth is for a sponsoring or "partner" church to give the money to pay the cost of construction of a big room on condition that within a decade, this congregation will give the cost of construction of an equal sized room to another new mission. (This in effect is a ten-year, no-interest loan geared to inflation.)

A sixth is to launch a new capital funds appeal to finance a second unit. This can be designed to focus on those who have joined since the last appeal and/or those who could increase their contributions if challenged. A seventh, if the change in interest rates makes this attractive and if the terms of the current mortgage permit it, is to refinance the remainder of the current mortgage plus the cost of a second unit in a new mortgage. The cost of this alternative usually will have much higher monthly debt service charges even if the term of the mortgage is extended.

An eighth, which has disadvantages as well as advantages, is to undertake a series of money-raising activities and/or pay part of the cost of that second unit from user fee charges collected for weekday use of that facility. (An adult day care or a weekday nursery school are two common examples.)

A ninth, which is more common in working class congregations, is for the members to construct that second unit with volunteer labor.

A tenth is for the denominational "church builders" crew to come in with a large cadre of volunteers and work with volunteers from that new mission in constructing the second unit.

An eleventh alternative, and one of the most widely followed, is to pay for that second unit out of the salaries not paid to the needed additional program staff. This can produce an attractive, but largely empty new building because of the absence of the additional staff to expand the program.

If, however, that mission developer is an unusually productive worker (and many are), if the vision called for building that new congregation as a collection of lay-owned and lay-operated organizations (see chapter 10), if the new mission has an excellent system for identifying, enlisting, training, placing, and supporting volunteers, and if numerical growth is continuing at a reasonable pace, this can be a useful alternative.

Finally, it may be possible to accommodate larger numbers of people through a revision of the schedule. This may include adding one or two worship experiences to the schedule, creating new teaching ministries during the week, running a double set of Sunday school classes, and spreading out the peak hour usage.

Municipal Restrictions on the Religious Use of Land

In an increasing number of communities the most complicated, the most frustration-producing, and the most expensive question facing new congregations is how to cope with restrictions of local public authorities on the religious use of land. While this is not the place for a treatise on constitutional law, five aspects of this will illustrate the complexity of the problem.[3] For several decades the courts have upheld statutes and ordinances that placed minimum requirements on improvements to the land. Thus it is easy to understand why a municipality would require a minimum of one hundred off-street parking spaces for a new church or require a minimum of 20,000 square feet of land for the site for a new church.

Recently, however, municipalities have been enforcing maximums. In one midwestern community the minimum number of off-street parking spaces was declared to be the maximum needed by that congregation and a request for a permit to expand the parking lot was denied. In several other communities the municipal government placed a maximum on the number of acres of land that any one church could own.

Back in 1954 a judge ruled in a landmark case, "The law is well settled that the building of a church may not be prohibited in a residential district." That led many to believe a church is a compatible use in a residential neighborhood. In recent years, however, both state and federal courts have supported the concept of special use districts for churches and/or supported municipal decisions barring churches from residential districts.

A third example is the Lakewood, Ohio, case in which the Sixth Circuit Court ruled that construction of a place of worship was a secular, not a religious, activity, and therefore the City of Lakewood could legally prohibit construction of a church building without violating the United States Constitution.

A fourth example is the increasing number of communities with laws to preserve landmark buildings that the courts have held are not in violation of either the first or fifth amendments to the United States Constitution.

A fifth is the creation of church-zoning districts and a congregation can build only in zoning districts that have been zoned to permit churches.

One of the expensive questions facing a growing number of new churches is, Do we surrender what we believe to be our

151

O, GIVE ME LAND, LOTS OF LAND...

It is easier to later sell surplus land than to expand our acreage!

—FRIAR TUCK

constitutional rights or do we spend the time and money to seek relief through the courts?

What Is a Good Site?

These increasing legal restrictions on the use of land lead into the fifth question. For decades such factors as location, availability, distance from other church buildings, access to utilities, size, accessibility, visibility, topography, subsoil conditions, drainage, and nearby land uses were the controlling factors.

In recent years two other questions have floated to the top of the list. What will it cost? Can we secure a building permit without a court fight?

The result is most new missions face a series of tradeoffs in choosing a new site. If we want a large site, we may have to pay more than we can afford. If we want accessibility, we may have to sacrifice visibility. If we want visibility and favorable topography, we may have to sacrifice location or accessibility.

What are the criteria that should be at the top of your list as you seek a site for a new church?

A reasonable case can be made for placing these eight near the top of that list:

1. Drainage and storm water control
2. Subsoil conditions
3. Access to public utilities including water
4. Size (almost always it is easier to sell surplus land than it is to expand the size of a site later)
5. Governmental restrictions on the use of land for religious purposes
6. Accessibility

7. Visibility

8. Location

At the bottom of that list probably should be distance from other church buildings unless you are in a community where nearly everyone walks to church.

What do you place at the top of your list? What tradeoffs are you willing to make?

Design Questions

One of the important tasks facing the congregation preparing to construct a new building is to find a competent architect who can comprehend their needs and design a structure to house both today's and tomorrow's congregations.[4]

The complexity of this issue can be illustrated by examining existing Protestant church buildings on the North American continent. The vast majority appear to have been designed with one or more of these assumptions in mind.

1. Most of the worshipers will walk and come first for worship so the main entrance should face the street.

2. Everyone attending will be comfortable climbing stairs, and most need the exercise.

3. Worship attendance will be approximately the same every Sunday week after week and year after year.

4. If and when this congregation decides to schedule two worship services for Sunday morning, each will attract approximately the same number of worshipers so it is not necessary to design a nave that can convey the impression it is comfortably full with two hundred people, but also can accommodate five hundred worshipers.

5. The seating capacity should be sufficient to accommodate everyone who may come to attend the memorial service for the beloved pastor who, after three or four decades of faithful service to that congregation, was assassinated by a deranged former member.

6. The nave and/or chancel and/or front entrance should provide an attractive photograph or line drawing for a bulletin cover or postcard.

7. The number of square feet required per person for people

seated at tables in the fellowship hall will be about the same as required per person for those seated in the nave.

8. All Sunday school classes will have the same attendance, so all rooms can be identical in shape and size.

9. The paid office staff will never include more than one or two ministers and one secretary.

10. It is dangerous to trust the next generation, so the building should be designed in a manner that will make it difficult or exorbitantly expensive for future generations to remodel or to enlarge.

11. Worshipers will leave their young children at home, so a nursery is unnecessary.

12. The biggest risk is a panic resulting from a fire, so the narthex should be tiny in order to facilitate getting people out in case of fire.

13. Most worshipers will either (a) be members of large families who worship together and/or (b) arrive early and prefer the middle of the pew so substantial economies can be achieved by using long pews.

14. Few events will last longer than two hours, so restroom accommodations can be modest.

15. People will use the corridors for pedestrian traffic only, never for fellowship or conversation, so money can be saved with narrow corridors.

16. Rarely will anyone drive by this building in an automobile, so identification of the congregation can be accomplished by a small bulletin board out front designed for pedestrians walking on this side of the street.

17. Modeling is not important, and children no longer are influenced by what they see adults doing, so classrooms for adults in the Sunday school can and should be at some distance from where the children meet for Sunday school.

18. Most people prefer wooden pews over upholstered chairs or theater-type seats.

19. Most pastors do not want to waste time greeting people after worship, so it is wise to provide several attractive, visible, and easily accessible exits from the nave.

20. Secrets are bad, so the pastor's study should not include an outside entrance. Any one coming to see the pastor should be

willing for the secretary and anyone else in the office to know about that visit.

21. Whenever that front door is unlocked, all parts of the building should be open to everyone rather than waste money by designing it as separate units that enable one to be locked while another is open.

22. Energy costs always will be low, so zoning for heating and cooling the building would be an extravagant luxury.

23. Only rarely will anyone ever come for the first time, so it is unnecessary to think in terms of a natural distribution of functions to make it easier for a first-time visitor to leave one place and find the next activity.

24. Choir members always prefer to rehearse in the same place they eventually will sing that anthem, so a separate choir rehearsal room is an extravagant and unnecessary luxury.

25. People are just as comfortable moving vertically as horizontally, so it would be extravagant to place the sanctuary and the fellowship hall on the same level.

While it is easy to ridicule yesterday, these examples do suggest a few criteria that can be used in the design of that permanent meeting place.

Perhaps the first on that list is the safest. Twenty years from now the people will want to do it differently, so design the new structure with an optimum degree of flexibility. One illustration is the design should offer at least three sharply different possibilities for expansion.[5]

The most significant question that will influence the design of that first "permanent" worship facility is the simplest to articulate. Will this be designed primarily for preaching? Or primarily for the proper administration of the sacraments?[6] Which priority reflects the central focus on how you want to express the faith?

A third question that should be central to the design of a new building or the remodeling of an older house of worship is more complex. What is it that we expect people will do when they come here and how can we help them do that in a meaningful way?

Perhaps the most obvious of the pragmatic questions to ask is will this place for corporate worship be designed so it can convey the impression of being comfortably full when attendance is only

NOW, LET'S SEE,
I THINK
THE CHURCH IS
SOMEWHERE
OVER THERE!

Getting to church
with small children is
a challenge which deserves
reserved parking spaces!
—FRIAR TUCK.

one-third of capacity? If it includes a balcony, a four-to-one ratio is an attainable goal.

A fifth consideration, which often is overlooked, concerns the use of volunteer labor. Many church buildings are designed on the assumption that all the construction will be completed by the contractor and subcontractors with paid crews. Other buildings are designed to facilitate the use of volunteer work crews. The size of that future mortgage can be reduced by $100,000 to $300,000 if the design makes it easy to turn to volunteer workers. This is an especially critical factor in those religious bodies that recruit volunteers from other congregations to help construct meeting houses for new missions.

Sixth, it usually is wise to place the fellowship hall on the same level with the sanctuary, separated perhaps by a corridor or the narthex in order to facilitate the movement of people from one room to the other.

Seventh, the corridors should be designed to encourage rather than stifle conversation and fellowship.

Eighth, it should be impossible to leave the nave by the principal entrance to that room without passing through a large space that facilitates the conversation and fellowship.

The additional exits from the nave and the chancel required by the fire code can be designed to be easily accessible in an emergency, but not as attractive as the exit that leads into that fellowship room.

Ninth, the entrance from the parking lot should be attractive and non-verbally suggest the direction for the stranger to go to worship or to find the office area or to go to the educational rooms or to the fellowship hall.

Tenth, the simplest way to provide the flexibility for an

increase in the program staff is to design the original plans with growth in mind. That future office space often serves as a meeting room for a decade more or less, but is easily adaptable to be part of the original office suite.

Eleventh, that office area should be a self-contained unit in terms of heating, cooling, security, access to restrooms, and, perhaps, to one general purpose meeting room.

Twelfth, the emphasis should be on designing attractive meeting rooms that can be used as classrooms rather than on designing classrooms that make second-class meeting rooms.

Thirteenth, the overall design should provide at least a dozen parking spaces reserved for visitors that are readily accessible to an attractive entrance to the building. In today's world it may be wise to provide several parking spaces close to the door leading into the nursery for single parent mothers. Getting to church on time with a one-year-old and a three-year-old is a big challenge that deserves a reserved parking space!

Fourteenth, the nursery should be designed (a) NOT to mix babies and eighteen-month-old children in the same room, (b) to be close to the major entrance from the parking lot, (c) to include a divided "dutch" door, (d) to have a wet sink with running water next to a counter that can be used for changing diapers, and (e) to have adequate storage for clothing, toys, diapers, name tags, and attendance materials.

Finally, the design for that first unit should include one large room that can house a Sunday school class taught by the pastor. This class should be an easy entry class that is both a learning experience for the participants and also an attractive entry point for timid inquirers who want to know more before deciding whether to make this their permanent church home.[7]

Although this is far from an exhaustive list of criteria for evaluating the design of that new building, it can serve as a beginning point. What else do you believe belongs on that list?

CHAPTER FOURTEEN

Why Is Continued Growth So Important?

Why do you place so much emphasis on numerical growth? Does a new church have to keep growing year after year to be a faithful and obedient servant of the Lord? What is wrong with leveling off on a plateau in size where we average one hundred fifty people, more or less, at Sunday morning worship? Why should we be expected to receive more new members every year than we lose? After all, a church of three hundred members has to receive at least a dozen to two dozen new members every year just to remain on a plateau in size. That maintains a steady flow of new faces coming in every year. What's wrong with concentrating our resources on quality, after we reach a size that is economically viable, rather than stressing quantity? Don't we have an obligation to feed the sheep rather than measuring everything by the size of the flock? Are we supposed to neglect or overlook all those who prefer to be part of a middle-sized parish that can minimize anonymity and maximize the creation of a loving, caring, supportive, and responsive fellowship of Christians? Why not start additional new missions out there rather than expect us to reach and serve everybody? Is there not an optimum size and when we pass that, the disadvantages outweigh the benefits?

These represent a few of the questions that frequently are raised when a new mission reaches the point of being a self-governing and self-financing congregation. One of the obvious explanations for many of these questions is simple. The typical congregation that begins with an attendance of sixty to one hundred tends to attract people who prefer being part of a small church. If they held strong preferences for a big church, they probably would not have joined this new mission. They liked what they saw, they became a part of it, why would anyone expect them to lobby vigorously to change what they wanted, what they helped create, and what they enjoy? Thus the frequent comment, "If I had wanted to be part of a big church, I would have joined one rather than coming here."

A related part of the explanation for these questions is substantial numerical growth almost always means substantial changes in the nature of that congregation, in the network of relationships, in schedules, in determining the priorities for the allocation of scarce resources such as money, building space, in the use of the pastor's time and energy, and in the style of ministry. If the people who helped pioneer what has become a financially self-supporting congregation now prefer stability to change, why expect them to change?

A dozen answers can be offered to those questions, but none of them may be overwhelmingly persuasive. The attraction of the status quo is more powerful than the call for change!

Why Grow?

The most obvious reason to insist on a never-ending effort to reach more people with the Good News about Jesus Christ can be traced back to the origins of most, but not all, new missions.

Although some were formed "to take care of our people who are moving here," in recent years most were started as a response to the Great Commission. That is a task that is never completed and that original purpose should continue to be at the heart of why that new mission exists.

Overlapping that is a second highly pragmatic reason. This is the subversion of goals.[1] Every institution is tempted, as the years go by, to subvert the original purpose by placing at the top of the

159

priority list institutional goals. One example is the natural and predictable tendency of educational institutions and municipal bus lines to make the students or bus riders the second priority. The top priority becomes taking care of the employees. The parallel is the new mission created to reach the unchurched soon begins to devote most of its resources to taking care of the churched, the membership. The best antidote is that continued effort to reach beyond today's membership.

A third reason is the frequently cited generalization, "A church either grows or declines, it can't remain on a plateau." Many exceptions exist to that generalization including most small congregations, some immigrant churches, and others, but it is a useful guideline. After year seven or eight of their existence, most new missions that average more than one hundred fifty people at worship do either grow in numbers or shrink in size. The numerical plateau rarely is a long-term viable alternative for the middle-sized-to-large church.

One of the most subtle reasons to push for continued numerical growth has an institutional, rather than an evangelistic, foundation. This is the tendency for growing organizations to be far more accepting than shrinking institutions of people who color outside the lines, of new ideas, of innovative leadership, of new people, and of new programs.

Overlapping this is the need in every organization for "new blood" as part of a larger goal of reaching and serving new generations. The numerically growing congregation is far more likely than the declining church to be able to attract and serve new generations of churchgoers.

A sixth reason is really an explanation. While exceptions do exist, in today's world an improvement in the quality of the ministries usually brings in many more people. Thus efforts to improve the quality of the ministry should be reinforced by the expectation that this will attract more people.

A seventh reason for growth has long-term implications. As a general rule, the larger the proportion of members who have joined within the past seven to ten years, the stronger the future orientation of that parish. The larger the proportion who have been members for a dozen or more years, the stronger the past orientation. New members help reinforce a future orientation.

Another pragmatic reason to encourage a positive attitude toward church growth is self-evaluation. One of the most meaningful and easy-to-measure yardsticks for evaluating the performance of any organization is to determine whether that organization can attract a new clientele. Perhaps the best single indicator for churches to look at is the number of people joining by letter of transfer. That is a good index to measure the effectiveness of any congregation in reaching that growing number of church shoppers. The number of people joining

BEING BIG ENOUGH GIVES ONE THE FREEDOM to SAY "NO"!

Large churches have enough volunteers to minimize burnout!
—FRIAR TUCK.

by letter of transfer is a good indicator of any one congregation's ability to compete with the other churches in that community for the growing number of church shoppers who are seeking quality.

Overlapping this is the biblical basis for self-evaluation. By definition every Christian congregation is charged with the responsibility of proclaiming the Word to the unchurched and of making new disciples for Christ.

A ninth reason is discretionary resources. Every organization benefits from the availability of discretionary resources. The growing organization is more likely to have discretionary resources than the shrinking institution where most resources are allocated to survival goals. In the church discretionary resources include the time and energy of volunteers, optimism, hope, money, staff, creativity, and physical facilities.

If the goal is to reach younger generations of adults, one of the assets in achieving that goal is to be able to offer people choices. The numerically growing church is far more likely to be able to offer people meaningful choices than the declining congregation.

An eleventh argument for numerical growth is that by

161

ALAS, CHURCHES WHICH REFUSE TO CHANGE DO CHANGE ...FOR THE WORSE!

WANTED: ANYONE TO BE OUR PASTOR

Non-growing churches have a tough time keeping energetic pastors!

—FRIAR TUCK.

definition the Christian faith is an extravagant religion. The number-one illustration of this is God's grace and God's love. The numerically growing church usually is able to reflect this extravagant dimension of the Christian faith more easily than the numerically declining congregation that tends to place a high priority on thrift, economy, and frugality.

Finally, a long pastorate often is a critical variable in the future of a new mission. While many exceptions do exist, as a general rule pastors of numerically declining missions or of churches on a plateau in size are more likely to be receptive to a call to greener pastures than ministers serving numerically growing congregations.

Are the pleas for remaining on a plateau in size more persuasive than the arguments for continued numerical growth?

CHAPTER FIFTEEN

A Denominational Perspective

The last six of the 44 questions to be discussed concern a half-dozen issues raised repeatedly by denominational leaders, as well as by the people in congregations who believe they are called by God to sponsor new missions. Some of these questions are far from simple, most are multi-faceted, and none are amenable to easy answers.

While this chapter has been written for denominational leaders responsible for new church development, parts of it may also be helpful to leaders in that growing number of megachurches who have decided to make church planting a high priority in that congregation's outreach and who are planning to start three-to-twenty new missions during the next decade.

Where and When?

Perhaps the first question to be raised and the one that recurs most frequently is, Where should we be allocating our scarce resources for new church development, when is the best time to enter a field, and how do we arrive at the answers to those questions?

The "where" question has several answers. The first is never plan to start a new church in any place unless you are absolutely convinced, without any reservations, that this new mission will add a distinctive facet to the larger effort to bring the Good News of Jesus Christ to every person in that area. Unless you have something to contribute, do not do it. Nearly every place on the North American continent has a surplus of redundant churches already. If your committee responsible for planting new churches cannot see how you could make a unique contribution to the religious scene in that community, do not plan to launch a new church there! Unless there is a compelling vision of what could and should happen (chapter 2), forget it.

Today many new churches are initiated by predominantly Anglo denominations as part of a larger goal of transforming that denomination into a multi-racial, multi-cultural, and multi-lingual religious body. That is vulnerable to the risk of using people for self-serving institutional grandizement. Avoid that!

The only valid motivation for starting any new churches is the combination of the Great Commission and a deep conviction that a new worshiping community related to our denominational family will reach people no other congregation will be able to reach and serve. Expansion of the denominational empire may or may not coincide with that vision. That is one reason that the possibility of the adoption of ethnic minority congregations by Anglo denominations (chapter 3) can turn into an ethical mine field.

This is not a serious problem for three groups of people active in planting new churches today. The easiest to identify are those who are convinced their religious movement is God's only instrument on this planet, all other churches are creations of the Devil, and therefore their churches are needed everywhere.

The second is the leaders in those independent churches who are not related to any larger institutional expression of the Christian Church and therefore do not have an empire that requires expansion.

The third, and potentially the largest, consists of those who are committed to what Peter Drucker identifies as the "pastoral churches" as their model for new church development. These are congregations designed to be sensitive and responsive to the religious needs of people. They are not franchises or branch outlets or retail facilities of a larger institution concerned about expanding its share of the market. The focus is on the religious needs of people, not on congregational or denominational goals.

Another perspective is to look at population movements. As a general pattern new churches tend to fill a need in those communities that are receiving large numbers of newcomers who do not express a strong kinship, religious, generational, nationality, racial, language, or cultural identification with the longtime residents. This should be examined in terms of population turnover, not simply net growth. Thus a county that will bid farewell to 20,000 residents this year and welcome 18,000 new residents may be a better place to start a new mission than the county that will bid farewell to only 500 residents, but will welcome 1,500 newcomers.

The key variable is not net growth. The key indicator is the number of newcomers who do not identify with the subculture of those remaining residents. This distinction can be seen most clearly in scores of inner city, older suburban, and rural areas that are experiencing (1) a net decrease in the total number of residents, (2) a rapid turnover in the population, (3) a shrinkage in the size of most of the long-established churches, and (4) a remarkable increase in the number of new congregations.

Too often policy makers responsible for planting new churches are mesmerized by that glittering identification of "high potential areas." This usually means these are zip code areas experiencing a rapid increase in the number of residents. One limitation of this vision is that it may overlook the high turnover areas described in the previous paragraph.

A second limitation is that these may not be areas of high potential numerical growth for the churches. The record makes it abundantly clear that population increases do not automatically produce membership growth for the churches.[1] A more realistic term would be to label these communities experiencing a rapid increase in population as "high competition areas." In most of them other people also are planting new churches. A reasonable assumption is that at least a few of these new missions will have the benefit of exceptionally competent ministers. This usually means they provide a highly competitive environment for both the existing congregations and also for those new missions with average or slightly above average quality pastors. Thus it is not uncommon for the lay leadership of long-established congregations in what is now labeled a "high potential" area to feel frustrated when their congregation does not experience rapid numerical growth. For similar reasons it is not surprising to find disappointed denominational leaders who had expected rapid growth in that new mission they planted in what is really a highly competitive ecclesiastical environment.

Overlapping this is the need to avoid being excessively influenced by the number of religious institutions in a given area. A far better indicator is to count the number of congregations that (1) were launched within the last eight years and are still experiencing numerical growth, (2) relocated their meeting place and constructed a new building within the past decade and/or, (3) enjoy exceptionally competent ministerial leadership. This often is the real competition for the allegiance of newcomers to that community. Many of the long-established congregations tend to be (a) heavily member-oriented and/or (b) primarily adult employment centers that provide jobs for clergy in need of income and/or (c) open only to those newcomers who are a cultural match and/or newcomers who come on their own initiative, usually as a result of strong denominational ties. All too often it is assumed that a church is a church is a church and a simple church-population ratio is the primary yardstick used to determine the need for new missions.

While it is far less significant than it was in the 1920s or 1950s, there remains a need to plant new congregations to "serve our people who are moving out there." This was and is a highly influential factor in the creation of new Roman Catholic parishes in suburbia, Christian Reformed Churches in Canada, Jewish synagogues, Cumberland Presbyterian churches, Lutheran Church-Missouri Synod missions, Church of Jesus Christ of Latter-Day Saints congregations, Southern Baptist missions, and new Seventh-Day Adventist churches. By contrast, in other religious bodies in which denominational loyalties have been severely eroded this may not be a powerful motivation.

Finally, a central facet of that "where" question is a product of the vision. If the vision calls for creating what will be relatively small family-centered congregations that are designed to attract neighbors who enjoy walking to church, a half-mile error in defining that "where" can be critical. Ideally this 1908 pre-automobile model of new church development will be located next to an elementary school (unless the local school system has decided to transport all children by bus as part of a strategy to implement other goals).

By contrast, if the vision calls for creating what will become a megachurch that will average at least a couple thousand at worship every week, the "where" will be defined by a different set of criteria based on a different set of assumptions about what society will look like in the year 2008. Among other criteria today's megachurch is created on the assumption that people will travel long distances two or three or four times weekly to have their religious needs met. Geographical convenience is far less influential than it was back in 1908. Megachurches flourish on the assumption that a high quality response to the religious needs of people is a more compelling factor in the choice of a church than is geographical convenience or denominational loyalty.

I HEAR 'EM COMING EVEN THOUGH THEY'RE TEN YEARS AWAY!

RELIGIOUSLY RESERVED

Today, denominations need to acquire building sites years in advance!

—FRIAR TUCK.

In other words, is the vision driving this venture in new church development based on recreating 1908 or on preparing for 2008?

When should we begin? The answer to that question includes several components. Plan to acquire land for future sites many years in advance! Do not begin before the first big wave of newcomers is beginning to arrive. Most significant of all, however, do not begin without an adequate inventory of competent church planters. The first pastor (or ministerial team) will shape that new mission (see chapter 2) so do not begin without (a) the vision of what you are seeking to create and (b) the minister you are convinced shares that vision and displays the gifts, skills, and personality required to turn that vision into reality.

The influence of the match between vision and church planter is illustrated by (a) the large and rapidly growing independent or semi-independent new missions in which the vision was the creation of that church planter and (b) the hundreds of small, struggling, and aging new missions in which the vision was generated by one party and another party selected the mission-developer pastor.

While it is extremely difficult to foresee, one other facet of that "where" question merits a brief mention.

One of the lessons of history is that new churches tend to excel in reaching newcomers. It matters little whether these are

With so many unchurched opportunity replaces competition!

—FRIAR TUCK

newcomers from another continent, another race, another generation, another region of the nation, another culture, another language, another social class, or another planet. Rarely are new missions successful in reaching large numbers of long-tenured residents unless the religious message carried by these new churches is one that literally and completely transforms all who come to hear and accept it.

When?

When should that new mission be launched? Ahead of the first wave of newcomers as part of a strategy to combine long-tenured residents and newcomers into one new reconciling fellowship? At or near the peak of that first wave? After the arrival of the first wave as part of a strategy to reach the second wave plus the replacements for people in that first wave who have moved on to another place of residence?

If the goal is to begin with a large initial core followed by rapid growth, the best time usually is near the peak of that first wave. If the strategy calls for long-term gradual growth, the best time may be near the beginning of the second wave.

Incidentally, this generalization probably has more relevance for new missions (a) in the inner city, (b) designed to reach immigrants from another continent, and (c) in exurban locations attracting the younger generations of newcomers than for upper-middle class and upper class suburbia.

In "high potential-high competition" suburban communities the key variable often is that initial vision. If that vision calls for sending in an average quality pastor with an average quality program, it may be wise to begin very early before the level of competition among the churches raises the quality of the long-established ministries and before many competing new missions are on the scene. If that average quality pastor arrives with an average quality program well after that second (or third) wave of growth has begun, the result often is disappointingly slow numerical growth.

If, however, that vision calls for sending in a top quality staff to build a megachurch, the best time may be at the peak of that first wave of population growth while large choice sites are still available and before the competition has become severe.

If turnover, rather than net population growth, is the prime contextual factor in deciding when and where to start a new congregation, and this often is the key variable in many suburban communities, the quality of the ministerial leadership should be the controlling force. In other words, in suburban communities experiencing an above average turnover in the population, it may be wise to postpone planting a new mission for a year or two or three if that delay will result in enlisting higher quality ministerial leadership than would be available earlier.

Who Initiates?

Should new missions be initiated by regional denominational executives? Or by pastors of long-established churches? Or by denominational committees? Or by an entrepreneurial minister who is compelled by that vision to act unilaterally? Or by a coalition of leaders, both lay and clergy, from local churches? Or by a national agency of that denomination that is able to formulate a set of national priorities? Or by an individual layperson who sees the need and can mobilize the necessary resources? Or by a Bible college or theological seminary committed to missions? Or by the women's organization either congregationally or regionally? Or by an interdenominational church planning agency or a council of churches?

Obviously local circumstances, tradition, polity, and the differences among leaders will influence this decision. From a denominational perspective, however, a strong argument can be made that a full-time specialist, perhaps with the advice and counsel of a supportive committee, will be charged with the responsibility, and given the authority to design a comprehensive strategy for that denomination. This strategy should include (1) defining and

169

ALAS, THERE GOES ANOTHER DENOMINATIONAL EXECUTIVE WHO DIDN'T KNOW *the* TERRITORY!

PARSON WORKING

Mobilizing local resources for church planting is a more efficient means of success!

—FRIAR TUCK

ranking in order the highest priorities by general location, (2) creating and maintaining a system for advance site acquisition, (3) devising a system for identifying, screening, enlisting, training, and placing mission-developer pastors, (4) designing a system for the enlistment of sponsoring churches, for creation of a lay church builders' club that will help finance new missions and for the organization and deployment of a group of volunteer construction teams, (5) offering expert consultation services to new congregations and, perhaps, (6) providing consultation services to long-established congregations that could and should relocate to become a new church for a new tomorrow in a new place.

For larger denominations the work load will be too great for one person and will require a professional staff.

If political and polity factors within that denomination require the involvement of regional judicatories and/or clusters of congregations in the places where new churches will be started, this normally will require the allocation of more money for paid staff in order to meet the additional needs for communication, coordination, attendance at meetings, and the smoothing down of ruffled feathers. Ideally, no more than 5 percent of all resources will be devoted to these institutional needs. If and when that proportion approaches 20 percent, consideration should be given to scrapping the existing system and replacing it.

One of the reasons for a highly centralized process is to make use of professional competence. This is especially important in site selection, timing, the selection of the mission-developer pastors, the choice of a model or style or approach to ministry for a particular new mission, oversight, and financing. The pressure for broad-based decision-making processes in new church development in recent years in several denominations may make this impossible. The conviction that one person's opinion should be as influential as the opinion of any outsider or denominational bureaucrat has turned out to be a remarkably effective means of creating relatively small and heavily subsidized new missions.

On the other hand, the larger regional judicatories organizing a half-dozen or more new churches every year probably can and should mobilize the resources within that regional judicatory rather than rely on a national agency for new church development. It does help to have the leadership of people who know the territory. A large regional judicatory can fulfill all six of those tasks described earlier including the necessary professional staff.

Perhaps the two most persuasive arguments for placing this package of responsibilities in a national agency are (1) the search for church planters may have to be a denomination-wide effort because of the shortage of skilled pastors for this specialized assignment, and (2) as urged earlier, the creation of that vision and the selection of the church planter should be housed in the same administrative place.

At the other end of the spectrum it is easy to identify five initiating points that have produced a disproportionately large number of disasters. One is the layperson who enlists a small cadre of people committed to starting a new church, gathers them for several months of weekly Bible study, acquires a site and/or a temporary meeting place, and subsequently secures a minister to become the pastor of what may have evolved into a small and often exclusionary lay-led fellowship.[2] That small number of highly visible success stories that have emerged from this initiating point have obscured the far larger number of disasters.

A second is the generous and mission-minded layperson who contributes a parcel of land, at his or her choice of location and size, if someone will build a new church on it.

A third is the associate minister of the large church who decides that an attractive exit from that increasingly unhappy role is to lead a small cadre of followers out to found a new mission that will be sponsored and financed by that large congregation.

A fourth is when considerable pressure is being felt to organize a new mission so one or two pastors plus a half-dozen lay leaders

171

from nearby churches accept (or take) the role of initiating leaders. They choose a site for the new mission in a location that almost guarantees the new mission (a) will not be an institutional threat or rival to the existing churches and (b) probably will have difficulty reaching as many as a hundred families during the first three years.

The fifth is when a denominational committee composed of representatives from various interest groups, factions, caucuses, geographical regions, and political parties is assigned the responsibility for devising a strategy for new church development and the determination of priorities. This design creates the temptation to focus on patronage, ideological considerations, and the choosing up of sides. This approach does illustrate the generalization that the greater the emphasis on participatory democracy in planning and decision making, the greater the probability that organization will repel the people it is seeking to reach.[3]

These five examples of less than perfect initiating points do illustrate the value of competence, skill, experience, objectivity, dedication, a strong future orientation, an ability to look at the larger picture, and the need to focus on the religious needs of newcomers rather than institutional priorities.

Enlisting and Training Church Planters

The Roman Catholic Church in the United States is experiencing a shortage of priests that may turn into a crisis. If it does, this probably will lead to the ordination of women and/or the elimination of the vow of chastity. The first incremental changes already have been taken toward what will be perceived as a radical change with (a) the assignment of nuns to serve as the resident pastors of small rural parishes and (b) the acceptance of married Episcopal clergymen into the Catholic priesthood.

The big shortages of pastors in American Protestantism appear to be (1) people who believe they have a call to a specialized vocation as a career associate minister, (2) ministers willing to serve rural churches in remote areas for a total compensation package that does not exceed 45 percent of the combined member contributions, (3) senior ministers willing to accept the role of initiating leaders in a large church, (4) pastors who are able and willing to serve as transformational leaders with congregations that need to redefine their role, and (5) skilled and effective church planters.

By contrast, the surplus is growing of ministers who seek a role as (1) the theologian-in-residence, (2) the co-pastor of a large church, (3) a counseling pastor, (4) the resident pastor with the responsibility of leading tours, and (5) the forty-hour-a-week pastor of a congregation able and willing to provide an above average compensation package.

From the very beginning God was thinking big!

— FRIAR TUCK

Among the incremental adjustments to these changes in the supply and demand of ministers are (1) a reduction in several denominations in the number of larger congregations, (2) an increase in the number of congregations that have shrunk to a size they no longer can either afford or justify a full-time resident pastor, (3) a sharp reduction in several denominations in the number of new churches started every year, (4) the closing or merger of at least 3,500 Protestant churches annually in North America—and that figure may be closer to 4,000, and (5) the turning to a wider variety of sources in the search for people to organize new missions, to serve as program staff members of larger churches, or to staff smaller congregations.

As was mentioned earlier, one of the critical variables in the strategy for enlisting church planters is the promise. What do you promise candidates to be mission-developer planters? Economic security for at least three years, a support system, assistance in purchasing the site for a permanent meeting place, and little accountability?

Or do you offer a challenge in the form of a vision, and minimal economic security, but lots of encouragement?

173

Which promise will attract the type of individual you are seeking?

A second critical variable is the distinction between the minister who reluctantly leaves a happy and effective pastorate in response to the attraction of that challenging vision, and the person who is so eager to leave an unhappy pastorate that any opportunity to move is attractive.

A third critical variable may be experience. Does the pastor who has had seven to twelve years of effective ministry in a numerically growing congregation have an advantage over the candidate who has served four pastorates, each in a numerically declining congregation? Or is the best choice the person with no previous parish experience who has nothing to unlearn and is eager to begin his or her pastoral ministry by pioneering a new church? (At least three dozen of the largest congregations on the North American continent were organized by ministers with no previous experience as parish pastors.)

The relevance of experience, and especially the relevance of experience in a large and rapidly growing congregation, can be illustrated by looking at what some contend are the most and least promising sources for pastors of new missions.

1. The senior minister of a congregation that now averages more than five hundred people at worship and has been experiencing numerical growth for this entire pastorate.

2. The minister who has had two happy and effective pastorates with numerically growing congregations, the second of which averaged at least two hundred at worship at that pastor's departure.

3. The team consisting of a pastor, an evangelist, and a program specialist or minister of music.

4. The church planter with only one pastorate, but that was in a new mission, it lasted at least six years, that congregation was averaging over two hundred at worship when that minister departed, and the members were unhappy when they discovered their minister was leaving.

5. The graduate of a Bible college. If the vision calls for building a megachurch, this alternative merits serious attention.

6. The promising seminary graduate who meets or exceeds all the criteria described later.

7. – 192. A range of 186 other possibilities.

174

193. The minister who has never served a numerically growing congregation that ever averaged more than one hundred twenty people at worship.

194. The minister who is exceptionally eager to terminate his or her present pastorate and either wants to or must leave as soon as possible.

195. The pastor who was dismissed by his or her last congregation, is currently unemployed, and needs a job.

196. The unemployed minister who was dismissed by his or her last secular or denominational employer and is seeking to return to the pastoral ministry.

A fourth critical variable is the recruitment process. Are the candidates nominated by other people such as the executives of regional judicatories, peers, and national leaders? Or does the process call for candidates to nominate themselves? Each has its advantages. Each is in effect a screening process. If this is perceived simply as a job in a bureaucratic or institutional setting, it may be appropriate to ask informed people to nominate candidates. If this is perceived as a challenge requiring an entrepreneurial, self-confident, self-directed, venturesome, future-oriented, and creative personality, it may be wise to encourage self-nominations.

Another way of stating this is to ask, Who will eliminate potential candidates from the list? Those doing the nominating? Or to create a process that means ministers eliminate themselves by not applying?

Which tests will be used to identify personality characteristics, entrepreneurial gifts, intellectual ability, and creativity? Or does the process not include the use of personality profiles or physical examinations?

If interviews are used in the screening process, will this be a carefully designed group interview in which the candidates compare themselves with one another? Or will these be one-on-one interviews between the selecting official and the individual candidates? Or both? Or will recommendations be used in place of interviews? If one-on-one interviews are used, will the interviewer be someone who has worked with at least a couple dozen church planters? Or will the interviewer be selected by virtue of office rather than expertise and experience?

If the concept of sponsoring churches is used, will the authority

175

THE NEED *to* ESCAPE A BAD SITUATION IS <u>NOT</u> A GOOD, NEW CHURCH-PLANTER'S QUALIFICATION!

—FRIAR TUCK·)

to select the church planter simply be delegated to the leaders in that sponsoring church, regardless of experience or expertise?

After three decades of experience with pastors of new congregations, this writer would urge the process include at least these eight components.[4]

1. A nation-wide search that includes *both* nominations by knowledgeable people *and* the opportunity for self-nomination.

2. At least five tests to measure extroversion-introversion, entrepreneurial gifts, creativity, intellectual ability, leadership initiative, and other personality characteristics.

3. At least four years of happy experience as a pastor of a numerically growing congregation.

4. Individual one-on-one interviews with each candidate utilizing the experience and skills of an interviewer who has had at least five years of experience in working with mission-developer pastors.

The competence of the interviewer is more important than denominational affiliation. If may be wise to turn to someone outside that denominational staff or regional judicatory in order to secure a qualified interviewer.

One of the reasons for this interview is to identify those who have an excessively romantic view of new church development. A second is to screen out those who simply are seeking an honorable exit from their present position.

A third reason for that interview is to screen out candidates who do not have a proven record in enlisting new members and/or who are uncomfortable or ineffective as fund raisers. A church planter should be able to motivate a generous level of financial support.

A fourth is to screen out those who do not feel they have a powerful call to the parish ministry as their Christian vocation. An introductory question on this issue may be, What do you see yourself doing ten years hence? While one of God's gifts to both human beings and cats is the ability to change one's mind, responses such as "seminary teacher," "bishop," "denominational staff position," or "associate minister on the staff of a large church" should provoke additional questions.

HE'S THE EXPERT at SURVIVAL in BOTH HOSTILE and UNCARING TERRITORIES!

The best interviewers of new church planters may not even be from our area or denomination!

—FRIAR TUCK⊙

5. Strong agreement by the candidate with and enthusiastic support of the vision that has been articulated for this particular new mission.

6. A group interview of five or six candidates for two hours conducted by an interviewer with considerable experience in group interviews. Three to five persons who will have a voice in making the final selection should be present as silent observers of this group interview.

7. Telephone calls, or better, face-to-face interviews with a half-dozen people who have firsthand knowledge of the candidate's experience, work record, character, and personality.

8. A physical examination for all candidates who reach the final stages of the selection process.

This is not a low cost process! The cost in terms of time, money, energy, and skill probably can be justified only by those who share the conviction that the selection of that minister is the most influential variable in determining the success of that new mission.

Today relatively few adults are employed as engineers, farm workers, accountants, aircraft mechanics, attorneys, retail clerks,

REMEMBER : THIS LAST JUMP IS JUST LIKE THE OTHERS ONLY HIGHER !

Training and experience are needed if new church planters are to flourish where they land !
—FRIAR TUCK

physicians, sanitation workers, teachers, receptionists, or plumbers without some on-the-job orientation or training immediately after appearing for work. One of the few exceptions to that is the parish ministry. It is widely assumed that ordination is such a powerful credential that on-the-job training is unnecessary for the newly arrived minister.

Those who challenge that assumption for church planters fall into four camps. One is composed of those who urge a five-to-thirty-day training program before going out to plant a new church. A second group includes those who believe experience-based training is more effective and argue that intensive training should follow after several weeks of experience in planting a new church, perhaps two or three months after arrival, but before the date is set for that first worship service.

The third group answers that before-or-after question with one word, "Both." This may take the form of an annual five-to-ten-day training event for church planters. Those who are about to embark on their first experience as church planters may come two days early or remain for three days after the close of that regular event to focus on their distinctive agenda. Part of the purpose for that annual event is to allow the inexperienced to learn from the veterans and to encourage the veterans to learn from one another.

The fourth group advocates the apprenticeship model. This calls for every prospective church planter to spend a minimum of ten to fifteen long days with an experienced and effective church planter as part of that screening process described earlier. Those who survive that apprenticeship are accepted and subsequently participate in that annual training event. (Those who advocate this apprenticeship model sometimes point out that a long unpaid apprenticeship is required of every applicant for a McDonald's franchise. Which is easier? To operate a profitable fast food restaurant? Or to organize a new church?)

What is your system for selecting and training pastors for new missions?

Can This Be a High Priority?

"The biggest priority we're facing is the rising cost of health insurance for our pastors," declared one denominational official. "The tax laws

mean we cannot expect the pastors to carry the costs; if they pay the premium most will receive few or no tax benefits. The tax laws place the burden on the employer, but most of our churches simply cannot afford to pay the entire premium. If we socialize the costs by paying it out of mission giving to our denomination, we won't have anything left for starting new churches."

"We just elected a new bishop for our regional judicatory who won because of the high priority he gave to social justice, peace, and urban issues. I don't believe our climate is supportive of new church development," remarked a leader from a different denomination.

"We're experiencing a lot of pressure to place a high priority on helping those churches of ours that have been shrinking in size to reverse that trend and to grow," commented an official from a third denomination. "That seems to be the top priority for us, and many of our people are convinced that starting a bunch of new churches will make it even more difficult for our declining churches to attract more members. They want help, not more competition."

* * *

While not everyone agrees with this diagnosis, an examination of those denominations that are experiencing significant numerical growth suggests the common variables are (1) starting new churches, (2) increasing the number of large churches, and (3) improving the quality of the preaching in long-established churches.

From a negative perspective two of these variables surface when an examination is conducted of those denominations that have been experiencing two decades or more of numerical shrinkage. Typically they have (1) reduced the number of new congregations organized each year and (2) reduced the number of large congregations.

The declining priority given to new church development can be illustrated by three sets of historical comparisons. In 1959 and 1960 the American Baptists organized a total of 76 new congregations; in 1969 and 1970 a total of 40; in 1979 and 1980 a total of 41. In 1959 and 1960 the two predecessor denominations of today's Presbyterian Church (U.S.A.) organized a total of 222 new churches; in 1969 and 1970 a total of 83 and in 1979 and 1980 a total of 124. In 1959 and 1960 the two predecessor denominations of The United Methodist Church organized a combined total of 357 new churches, in 1969 and 1970 a total of 44 and in 1979 and 1980 a total of 190. By contrast the Southern Baptist Convention organized a total of 620 new congregations in 1969 and 1970, a total of 798 in 1979 and 1980, and a total of 876 in 1987 and 1988. Do those numbers suggest a change in priorities?

One reason, of course, for this decline in several denominations is that conventional approaches to new church development require more money. Between 1955 and 1990 land costs (in constant dollars) increased thirty times, the cost of money (interest rates) nearly doubled and construction costs (again after allowing for inflation) nearly doubled. That is one set of reasons why it is unrealistic to attempt to perpetuate the 1955 models of new church development!

These four paragraphs stand out as a reminder of a fact of denominational decision making that often is overlooked. Three words that frequently go together are rational, logical, and irrelevant.

A Denominational Perspective

If logic and rationality are not the roads to follow to make new church development a high priority, what it?

Two answers can be given to that question. One is religious. The other is institutional. The better of the two is the strong and widely shared evangelistic conviction that planting new churches is operationally the most effective means of implementing the Great Commission. The absence of such a conviction will make it difficult to mobilize the resources necessary for an aggressive program of new church development. The absence of such a

NEW CHURCHES ARE A FAD OF THE PAST!

Without a new church priority, most denominations languish in lethargy! —FRIAR TUCK

conviction makes it easier to place the institutional survival of existing churches at or near the top of the priority list. The temptation to allocate resources to the dying rather than giving birth to the new is a normal, predictable, and natural tendency in every aging institution. How much money is allocated for health insurance and pensions? How much staff time is allocated to those two concerns? How much money and how much staff time is allocated to giving birth to new churches? How much money does our society allocate to the care and the comfort of the elderly? How much to the care of infants and young children? On a per capita basis eleven times as many federal dollars go to the elderly as go to children in the United States.

In both examples the same two questions can be asked? Who votes? Who will constitute the future? The past usually casts more votes than the future, but the future is with the young.

The other answer to this issue of making new church development a high priority in your denomination or regional judicatory comes out of studies of organizational dynamics. This answer is to make this the *only* responsibility of a full-time, goal-driven, competent, committed, persistent, determined,

181

LEFT ALONE, SHE COULD PROBABLY WALK ON WATER!

NEW CHURCH DEVELOPER
MS. ITCANBEDONE

ENTER WITH ENTHUSIASM!

New church development needs an enthusiastic staff person with only that responsibility!

—FRIAR TUCK.

task-oriented, visionary, creative, tenacious, optimistic, articulate, persuasive, dogged, skilled, and credible staff person who either has earned or can earn the respect of those who influence policy formulation. That staff person MUST have the freedom to build a support group for this priority. That includes the authority to enlist individuals as members of a church builders' club or as volunteers on a construction crew, to recruit "partner" or "sponsoring" churches, to acquire sites in advance, to have an influential voice in the selection, training, placement, and oversight of all mission-developer pastors, and to determine the timing for starting a new mission in a specific place.

In many cases this individual will need staff assistance. Rather than place one staff person for new church development in each of the two or three regional and national layers of that denominational bureaucracy, it may be wiser to concentrate those resources in this one office.

Ideally, of course, this staff leader, all others on that staff, and all members of the support committee will be driven by the categorical wording of the Great Commission. (Ideally this staff leader will be accountable to this committee, not to a complex bureaucratic structure.)

The alternative of assigning new church development to one central agency that has a variety of responsibilities usually turns out to be an effective means of making this a relatively low priority for that denomination. If the goal is to keep it as a low priority, that can be achieved by making it the part-time responsibility of a subordinate staff person who also carries two or three other portfolios, one of which is more attractive to that subordinate than new church development.

A Denominational Perspective

How Many?

"We're starting about half as many new churches each year as we did back in the 1950s," reflected one denominational official, "and I'm afraid that's not enough."

"I wish we were doing that well," declared someone from a different denomination. "We're starting about a fourth as many as we did in the 1950s."

* * *

How many new churches should your denomination be

> NOW LET'S SEE, WE'LL START WITH A WEEK of PREACHING, THEN WE WILL LOOK FOR A BUILDING SITE...

> STARTING A NEW CHURCH

> In the last century, each denomination grew in ratio to its number of new churches!
>
> —FRIAR TUCK

organizing every year? One beginning point is to compare the current total with your peak years. Is it up or down?

A second is to divide the estimated financial resources by the average cost of each new mission and come out with a bookkeeping figure. This is almost always one of the most effective techniques for keeping that number low.

A third is to determine the number of new churches to be launched by the potential number of competent, interested, and available church planters. That may be the second or third most effective means of minimizing that numerical goal.

A rational analysis of available resources almost always understates the potential capability of any individual, organization, congregation, or denomination.

A fourth is to set a single, numerical goal based on last year's statistics. This is to count the number of congregations that closed, disbanded, disappeared via merger, were dissolved or left the denomination last year. Add the number one or the number two to that total in determining how many new churches will have to be started in order to remain on a plateau. Thus if you experienced the loss of ten congregations last year, plan to launch eleven or twelve new ones this year. This is a replacement goal.

183

A fifth is more complicated. This is based on the generalization that in numerically growing denominations at least 20 percent of all churches were organized during the past quarter century. (In several of today's rapidly growing religious bodies that figure is between 35 and 60 percent.) How many of your present churches are less than fifteen years old? How many new churches will you have to organize in the next decade so that ten years hence at least one-fifth of your congregations will be less than twenty-five years old? What will be the annual figure to achieve that ten-year goal? Remember, many new congregations do not survive as long as their twenty-fifth birthday.

A simpler yardstick is to multiply the present number of congregations in your denomination or regional judicatory by 0.8 percent. On the average about 0.8 percent of all Protestant churches in North America need to be replaced every year to offset those that close, leave the denomination, disband, disappear via merger, or move into the terminally ill stage of their institutional life.* Can you calculate that annual average for your denomination over the past two decades? Can that help you formulate a numerical goal? Is your goal to reduce the rate of numerical decline? If so, that 0.8 figure may be the quantified objective. If the goal is to grow, use the 1 percent goal described in the "Introduction" to this book.

A seventh numerical goal could be a response to this question. Based on past experiences, approximately 5,000 to 6,000 new Protestant churches will be started in the United States next year. What is our share of that figure? Is it 1 percent? Two percent? Three percent? Ten percent? What percentage of the estimated 350,000 Protestant churches in the United States are affiliated with your denomination or your regional judicatory?

Perhaps the best beginning point is to respond to this question, What do we believe the Lord is calling us to do? How do we translate that call into specific plans for new churches?

---

*In Iowa, for example, the number of congregations affiliated with The United Methodist Church or one of its predecessor bodies dropped from 2,031 in 1906 to 900 in 1986. The number affiliated with the United Church of Christ and its predecessor denominations dropped from 422 in 1906 to 210 in 1987. The number of Episcopal parishes in Iowa declined from 91 in 1906 to 70 in 1980. The population of Iowa grew from 2,225,000 in 1906 to 2,851,000 in 1986.

A Denominational Perspective

Who Delivers the Bad News?

One of the sad facts of life is that not everything works as planned. That generalization also applies to new churches. Some become outstanding success stories. Others plateau prematurely. A few die young.

Sometimes, denominational vision and intervention can redeem a static situation!

One of the difficulties that sponsoring congregations often encounter when they decide to plant new missions is in providing unsolicited intervention. If that new mission begins to encounter difficulties in year three or four, how does the sponsoring or mother church intervene? Sometimes with the same welcome a mother receives in offering unsolicited advice to a seventeen-year-old daughter or son.

This is one of the more persuasive arguments in building a continuing oversight responsibility into the national office or regional judicatory of the sponsoring denomination. The easiest, but not necessarily the best way to accomplish this is to tie a periodic review to that annual financial subsidy. A better way may be to structure this right of intervention into the original agreement for the launching of this new mission. United Methodist, Presbyterian, and Roman Catholic polity make this easy to accomplish. It is far more difficult in the pure congregational polity. There the acceptance of unsolicited outsider intervention often is determined by the personality and competence of that denominational staff person.

Perhaps the most difficult point of unilateral intervention, and also one of the two most serious, is when it becomes apparent the mission-developer pastor is not a good match for that situation. This may be a product of the selection process or of human error or of the simple fact that people do change. Three of the most common symptoms of the mismatch are (1) several pioneers drop

IT WOULD'VE BEEN *an* ERROR
HAD ABRAHAM *and* SARAH
STAYED *in* UR !

With more than
5,000 new churches
starting each year,
can we afford to start none?

— FRIAR TUCK

out and/or go to some other church, (2) first-time visitors do not return, and (3) a never-ending financial crisis always is at the top of that agenda.

Who delivers the bad news to that pastor that the time has come to move on to another task?

A different and more common version of the same issue is when those pioneer volunteer leaders and the mission-developer pastor agree that the goal is to build this congregation as a loving, caring, and supportive network of one-to-one relationships with the pastor at the hub of that system. The problem arises, however, when it turns out the productivity level of this pastor means that congregation will never move beyond seventy to a hundred people at worship and the vision called for this to be a much larger congregation. Who intervenes and how?

Other points of potential intervention include when (1) the site chosen earlier for a permanent meeting turns out to be inadequate, below standards, or poorly located, (2) the time has arrived to move forth out of the comfort of that low cost temporary meeting place but the new mission needs a push to do it, (3) care of the members begins to take more than 70 percent of the pastor's time and energy (this may be the signal for a reallocation of priorities on the pastor's time or it may be the signal for adding staff), (4) the building planning committee becomes enamored with what clearly is a bad or extravagant design for that first unit, (5) the level of member giving plateaus or drops, (6) moral charges are leveled against the pastor, (7) the expansion of the group life and/or program plateaus, (8) disruptive conflict erupts between the pastor and the volunteer leadership, (9) the frequency of attendance begins to drop and/or the average attendance in the Sunday school begins to decline, (10) someone suggests the easy solution to the current financial crisis would be to sell part of the land, (11) a former pastor returns frequently to conduct weddings and funerals, and (12) the total compensation for the pastor exceeds 50 percent of total member giving.

Finally, what may be the most painful point of intervention is when the facts suggest this new mission should be disbanded. In some cases this is because the population projections that motivated the vision were not fulfilled. In

other new missions changes in land use patterns mean this no longer is a promising location. In at least a few the primary reason the balloon did not go up can be traced back to unfortunate choices in selecting that initial cadre of volunteer leaders. (See chapter 11.) In others two or three consecutive mismatches between minister and mission have so undercut morale, damaged the community image, and encouraged scapegoating that a minor miracle would be needed to salvage the situation. In several cases the new mission turned out to be a weak, underfinanced, underprogrammed, and redundant clone of a larger congregation nearby.

Sometimes the wise course of action is to disband the present congregation and wait a year to make a fresh start with new leadership. Not infrequently the decision has been to sell the assets to another church from a different religious orientation. In others the decision was to merge the tiny new mission with an older congregation seeking an excuse to relocate. A few of these "bail outs" have been successful, but they usually require exceptionally competent ministerial leadership.

Experience suggests (1) it may be wise to intervene early, rather than wait until a significant number of frustrated volunteers have left, (2) a minimum of two, and perhaps three or four intervention meetings will be needed in order to give the volunteer leaders a chance to reflect on alternatives, talk with one another, and express their second thoughts, (3) the same outsider should be present at every intervention on any one subject, (4) asking questions and active listening can be an effective style of intervention, (5) whenever possible, people should be offered realistic alternative courses of action, (6) formal voting should be postponed until after a consensus has emerged, and (7) once the intervention process is underway, patience can be a valuable virtue.

While it is unrealistic to hope to eliminate all risks in new church development, careful attention to these six questions can reduce those risks substantially.[5]

Notes

Chapter One

1. Edwin Scott Gustad, *Historical Atlas of Religion in America* (New York: Harper & Row, 1962), p. 43.
2. *Ibid.*
3. Bureau of the Census, *Religious Bodies: 1906* (Washington: Government Printing Office, 1910), Part I, pp. 22-99.
4. An interesting, but mildly controversial discussion of the increase in entropy is Jeremy Rifkin, *Entropy* (New York: Viking Press, 1980), pp. 33-96.
5. For a scholarly analysis of social development, see Robert A. Nisbet, *Social Change and History* (New York: Oxford University Press, 1969).
6. The probability that new churches are more likely to experience numerical growth than long-established congregations has been confirmed by dozens of denominational studies. One of the very best of these research monographs is C. Kirk Hadaway, *New Churches and Church Growth in the Southern Baptist Convention* (Nashville: Broadman Press, 1987).
7. For one of many advocates of the house church, see Del Birkey, *The House Church: A Model for Renewing the Church* (Scottdale, Pa.: Herald Press, 1988). For a sympathetic and exceptionally thorough evaluation of the house church concept, see Kirk Hadaway, et al., *Home Cell Groups and House Churches* (Nashville: Broadman Press, 1987).
8. A discussion of comity, including its limitations, can be found in Lyle E. Schaller, *Planning for Protestantism in Urban America* (Nashville: Abingdon Press, 1965), pp. 96-112.
9. For an introduction to this constitutional debate, see Scott David Godshall, "Land Use Regulation and the Free Exercise Clause," *Columbia Law Review*, vol. 84, October 1984, pp. 1562-89.

Chapter Three

1. Bureau of the Census, *Religious Bodies: 1906* (Washington: Government Printing Office, 1910), Part I, p. 25.
2. A brief but lucid and example-filled argument for "parenting" new churches can be found in Ray Harsh, "How Can Your Church Parent a New Church?" *Baptist Herald*, May 1989, pp. 10-11, and Bernard Fritzke, "How a Church Planting Project Benefits from a Mother Church," *Ibid.*, p. 12.

Chapter Five

1. For an extended discussion of the importance of place in people's lives, see Lyle E. Schaller, *Effective Church Planning* (Nashville: Abingdon Press, 1979), pp. 65-92.

Chapter Six

1. A more extensive description of these and other approaches to ministry can be found in Lyle E. Schaller, *Choices for Churches* (Nashville: Abingdon Press, 1990), chapter 1.
2. Several of the reasons behind these limitations on numerical growth are described in Lyle E. Schaller, *Looking in the Mirror* (Nashville: Abingdon Press, 1984), chapter 1.

Chapter Seven

1. For what is still the best definition of the homogeneous unit principle, see C. Peter Wagner, *Our Kind of People* (Atlanta: John Knox Press, 1979). See also C. Peter Wagner, ed., *Church Growth: State of the Art* (Wheaton, Ill.: Tyndale House Publishers, 1986), pp. 17-18, 34.
2. One example of an attempt to blend these three components with the dynamics of small groups is described in James A. Christopher, *Gifts Believers Seek* (New York: Pilgrim Press, 1988).
3. An exceptional description of this distinction can be found in Margaret M. Poloma, *The Assemblies of God at the Crossroads* (Knoxville: University of Tennessee Press, 1989). This conflict between a focus on the rational and intellectual approach to Christianity versus a simple faith approach has been a divisive force for centuries. The impact of this tension on the church-related university is described in a delightful essay by James Nuenchterlein, "Athens and Jerusalem in Indiana," *The American Scholar*, Summer 1988, pp. 353-68.
4. An excellent model for building on growth groups is Charles M. Olsen, *Cultivating Religious Growth Groups* (Philadelphia: Westminster Press, 1984).
5. While it does display a bias that will offend some people, a useful resource on the state of the family in the United States is the monthly, *The Family in America.* For subscription information write P.O. Box 416, Mount Morris, Ill. 61054. (The bias is a strong marriage, pro-family, anti-divorce, pro-child orientation that includes the assumption people must live with the consequences of their actions.)

Chapter Nine

1. Walter Mueller, *Direct Mail Ministry* (Nashville: Abingdon Press, 1989).
2. "The American Way of Buying: A Wall Street Journal Centennial Survey," *Wall Street Journal*, November 6, 1989.

Chapter Eleven

1. Frances Fitzgerald, *Cities on a Hill* (New York: Simon & Schuster, 1983), pp. 203-45 ff, or Lyle E. Schaller, *Expanding Ministries with Retirees, Seasonal Visitors, and Tourists* (New York: United Church Board of Homeland Ministries, 1987).
2. See Lyle E. Schaller, *The Multiple Staff and the Larger Church* (Nashville: Abingdon Press, 1980), pp. 15-50.
3. See Lyle E. Schaller, *Choices for Churches* (Nashville: Abingdon Press, 1990), chapter 1.

190

Notes

Chapter Thirteen

1. For an extensive discussion of the importance of place in people's lives, see Lyle E. Schaller, *Effective Church Planning* (Nashville: Abingdon Press, 1979), pp. 65-92.

2. For a discussion of the need for more space to accommodate the same number of people, look at the size of the new single family homes being constructed today or the parking lot at the local high school or see Lyle E. Schaller, *Reflections of a Contrarian* (Nashville: Abingdon Press, 1989), pp. 109-22.

3. A useful introduction to the problem with the citation of relevant cases is Scott David Godshall. "Land Use Regulation and the Free Exercise Clause," *Columbia Law Review,* vol. 84, October 1984, pp. 1562-89. While it does not speak to the zoning question, an excellent description of the confusion in judicial opinions on the interpretation of the establishment clause is Leonard W. Levy, *The Establishment Clause* (New York: MacMillan Publishing Co., 1986).

4. Useful advice on this can be found in Edward A. Sovik, "An Orderly Journey: The Processes of Environment and Art," *Reformed Liturgy & Music,* vol. XXII, Spring 1988, pp. 78-85. Sovik has earned a reputation as one of the two or three most distinguished church architects in North America. His office is in Northfield, Minnesota. The Division of Evangelism and Local Church Development of the United Church Board for Homeland Ministries has produced an excellent manual and a superb set of video tapes for use by congregational building committees.

5. A series of seventy-eight questions for the building planning committee are suggested in Lyle E. Schaller, *Looking in the Mirror* (Nashville: Abingdon Press, 1984), pp. 190-200.

6. An excellent brief discussion on this preaching or sacramental priority is James F. White, "Liturgical Space Forms Faith," *Reformed Liturgy & Music,* vol. XXII, Spring 1988, pp. 59-60. That same issue also contains an outstanding article by S. Anita Stauffer, "Theology and Worship Space: Some Reflections" and "A House for the American Church" by Susan J. White.

7. One model of the pastor's class is described by Lyle E. Schaller, *The Senior Minister* (Nashville: Abingdon Press, 1988), pp. 146-48.

Chapter Fourteen

1. Donald L. Metz, *New Congregations* (Philadelphia: Westminster Press, 1967).

Chapter Fifteen

1. Lyle E. Schaller, *Reflections of a Contrarian* (Nashville: Abingdon Press, 1989), pp. 96-108.

2. For a longer discussion of this syndrome, see Lyle E. Schaller, *Survival Tactics in the Parish* (Nashville: Abingdon Press, 1977), pp. 69-75.

3. Lyle E. Schaller, *Getting Things Done* (Nashville: Abingdon Press, 1986), chapter 5. All the other good outcomes of this initiating point are summarized on page 843 of this book.

4. Another perspective for defining the characteristics of a good church planter can be found in Lyle E. Schaller, *Growing Plans* (Nashville: Abingdon Press, 1983), pp. 135-38.

5. A scholarly and original examination of the management of risk is Aaron Wildavsky, *Searching for Safety* (New Brunswick, N.J.: Transaction Publishers, 1988). The author repeatedly makes the point that excessive caution often reduces safety and increases the probability of undesired results. One moral from this book is that redundancy is more effective than caution or efficiency in any effort to reach more people with the Good News about Jesus Christ.